ECONOMIC AND SOCIAL COMMISSION FOR ASIA AND THE PACIFIC

TRAFFIC AND TRANSPORTATION FOR SUSTAINABLE ENVIRONMENT, MOBILITY AND ACCESS

Application of a Comprehensive and Integrated Approach to Policy Development in the Rattanakosin Area of Bangkok

Executed in cooperation with

Bangkok Metropolitan Administration

UNITED NATIONS
New York, 2001

This study was undertaken with the assistance of

The Royal Netherlands Government

ST/ESCAP/2171

UNITED NATIONS PUBLICATION
Sales No. E.02.II.F.27
Copyright © United Nations 2001
ISBN: 92-1-120087-3

ESCAP WORKS TOWRDS REDUCING POVERTY
AND MANAGING GLOBALIZATION

Preface

It is now recognized that transport policies and plans produced through the traditional top-down approach tend to over-emphasize the supply-side traffic engineering solutions, while ignoring the importance and cost effectiveness of demand management and other approaches which are more participatory in nature. There have been numerous studies on the well-known traffic and transportation problems of Bangkok. Some of them were quite comprehensive in nature and others more focussed on some specific problems. However, all of them had something in common – they were based on the traditional top-down approach and the proposed solutions reflected largely professional points of view. The policy prescriptions of these studies lacked general public support and authorities failed to implement many of the crucial "hard" choices. As a result, despite many efforts made in the past, the severity of the problems still exists. In contrast to the limitations of the traditional approach, lessons drawn from many places around the world suggest that a "bottom-up" participatory approach is more likely to win public support especially when the questions of difficult policy choices and public actions arise. Encouraged by its success, participatory approaches to planning and development have been institutionalised in many countries with applications in different fields of development.

Considering the potentials for success of a participatory approach, particularly for policy choices involving harder issues, the Rattanakosin Project was conceived as a pilot project aimed at 1) making specific contributions to the overall solutions of the traffic and transportation problems in the area, and 2) to share the lessons learned about this approach with other countries in the region. The pilot project was executed by the United Nation's Economic and Social Council for Asia and the Pacific (UN ESCAP) in coorperation with Bangkok Metropolitan Administration (BMA) and with financial and technical support from the Royal Netherlands Government. In the course of undertaking the project a number of important lessons have been learned, at least two of which deserve detailed consideration.

First, the merits of participatory approaches have been recognized by stakeholders and consideration needs to be given to introducing them as effective approaches to all future planning exercises in Bangkok. However, this would require institutional development in many areas ranging from the organization of the participatory process itself, to changes in the functional structure of BMA to facilitate practicing of these approaches. Second, professional expertise has developed within the project team in analysing and structuring the views and suggestions of stakeholders to develop an integrated and comprehensive package of actions, which can be shared by other cities in the region.

After an introductory section, the report, therefore, has been organized in two main parts, namely, institutional development and "technical" actions, both of which are based on views expressed by the project's stakeholders. The first part concerns actions to institutionalise participatory approaches to planning and development in BMA. It outlines various issues related to institutional development that would be required to address the successful introduction of participatory approaches in the planning process. The first part also reviews the standing of participatory approaches in general within the broader contexts of constitutional provisions and the on-going reorganization of local government functions in Thailand. The second part of the report deals with specific actions for consideration that could be undertaken to address some of the major issues and problems mainly related to traffic and transportation in Rattanakosin. This part contains twelve integrated action plans to deal with the identified major issues in transportation in a comprehensive and integrated manner.

Generous support and cooperation have been received from the Royal Netherlands Government and the concerned stakeholders without which it would not have been possible to undertake and complete the project. Mention must be made of the stakeholders who happened to be the kingpins of this project. Their whole-hearted support, deep interest, and untiring participation in long workshops testify people's confidence in participatory approaches and also their willingness to get involved in the planning and decision-making process. With their support, it should be much easier for the authorities to consider implementation of the "hard" choices and thereby could go a long way towards sustainable development in Rattanakosin.

CONTENTS

Page

LIST OF TABLES

LIST OF FIGURES

INTRODUCTION

It could be ironical or congruous or both, depending on one's outlook, that with the advancement of knowledge and technology, more and more problems have come in view. In many developing countries increasing numbers of people have come to live in cities, as a better alternative to rural hardship. The rapid growth of cities has led to massive demand for transportation and other urban services. However, the pace of development in those sectors could hardly match the increasing demand for such services. Consequently, transportation and other urban-related problems have been increasingly aggravated. Infrastructure for motorized transport has been constructed for speedy travelling. However, with the apparently unlimited increase in the number of motor vehicles, the benefits of additional road capacities start to disappear very quickly. Elevated expressways often become parking lots in the sky. The examples are numerous. Yesterday's solutions turn out to be today's problems. Transport related and general urban problems seem to be not only omnipresent, but also never ending.

Knowledge about the urban crisis has become a subject of common awareness in the public domain. "…the vast spread of squatter settlements and shanty towns, ill supplied, if at all, with basic amenities…rapid environmental deterioration, giant traffic jams, violence and crime, urban sprawl eating into the countryside, these are some of the most striking visible features of the growth of large cities in developing countries…".[1] A statement depicting the urban crisis of this kind, so common nowadays hardly needs further elaboration.

Transportation in Bangkok is a good case in point. Within the span of half of a century Bangkok has completely lost its image as "Venice of the East". It is now notorious for its traffic and transport problems, and is being associated with one of the top, if not the top of the list, of the world's most traffic-congested cities. The level of road congestion is brimming full to the point that any extra unfavourable event could grind traffic to a standstill for a considerable part of a day. The canals, which were once the arteries of communication, have been bridged or decked over to make way for motorized road transport, miserably polluted and in many cases become unnavigable. With problems on top of those arising from transport, lives in Bangkok are ravaged with inconveniences and discomforts of various kinds. They impose incalculable costs to all aspects of life. This is true for most social and income groups.

Correspondingly, attempts to address the problems have accumulated. Solutions from both the demand and supply sides have been proposed. Some have been implemented, some are in the process of implementation and others are under consideration. In addition to the proposed solutions, there have been numerous studies on the problems of urban development in general and of traffic in particular. These studies and proposed plans are extensive[2], both in quantitative and qualitative terms, so much so that the search for solutions has virtually left no stones unturned. It is often claimed that any seemingly new solution will likely bear certain similarities with those in the stock.[3] However these ideas are largely, if not purely, derived from the professional and bureaucratic points of views.

Many of those proposed solutions have had difficulties in implementation. One of the prominent reasons for these difficulties has been the fact that the approaches used in developing them have been principally of top-down in nature. The approaches have tended to overlook the "popular perception of project practicalities"; hence they seriously lacked a necessary broad-based consensus, let alone support. People are, as a matter of virtue and of fact, "idea benefactors" and "direct beneficiaries", and they need to be recognised as such.

1

When people have been marginalized or even ignored, ideas and plans, irrespective of their values, have frequently been incapacitated. Therefore the issue of people's involvement is being increasingly appreciated as a very critical element for the success or failure of development projects.

Ample experiences in developmental efforts in the recent decades both in the rural and urban contexts have pointed, on the one hand, to the limitations of top-down approaches, and on the other hand, to a higher degree of success of participatory approaches. Theoretically, as well as evidently, policies and projects are likely to be more successful, if they are receptive to collective efforts from the public and the community, and not just left to the market mechanism or bureaucratic management. The merits of this outlook have been underscored in many parts of the world. That is why a statement like "People's participation is becoming the central issue of our time" has often been quoted[4]. Terms like participatory approaches, people's participation, community participation, stakeholders' participation, though having different connotations, have gained general acceptance by the civil society. And more and more they have been put into practices in various spheres and in different contexts.

The concept of people's participation is also very keenly adhered to in the context of Thailand. With the trend towards democratic ideas at the global level in general and at the national level in Thailand in particular, the principle of participation has been well integrated into Thai public life for a considerable period of time. As enshrined in the supreme law, the Constitution of 1997, Section 76 stipulates: "The State shall promote and encourage public participation in laying down policies, making decision on political issues, preparing economic, social and political development plans, and inspecting the exercise of State power at all levels." Before the constitutional recognition, the concept of people's participation has long been propounded and given a special status in the development process in the official arena of both planning organizations as well as of functional agencies. The National Economic and Social Development Board (NESDB) Plans since the Fifth Plan (1982–1986) and the Fifth Bangkok Metropolitan Development Plan (1997-2001) are but two direct cases in point, not to mention civic bodies and international organizations namely the United Nations that have advocated and promoted people's participation all along.

The rationale as well as the practice of election from the village to the provincial level and the general election has been well understood and upheld as a working principle. The election at different levels, however, is a specific kind of participation. The principle has long been extended to arena other than the political. Rural development is a good case in point. A large proportion of villagers all over the country has been familiar with and is taking part directly in the participatory process.[5]

The process has not been alien in the urban areas either. Great successes have been achieved both at the community and the city level. Owing to the traditional spirit and long establishment of communities, urban dwellers in many parts of Bangkok and other major provincial cities have made significant strides in addressing urban ecological issues. Waste management, for example, has been a common concern and receives contributions without which it could have been in a much worse situation.

At the city level, an example directly concerned with the traffic and urban problems can be cited from two popular radio programmes, namely, *Jor Sor 100* (now a household name on FM radio) and *Ruam Duay Chuay Kan* (literally "Together we can help each other"). They are increasingly popular 'phone-in' type of radio programmes whereby people make phone calls to report the traffic situation they are witnessing from the spot. They also report accidents on the roads and other events that could affect traffic movements. Regularly the announcers phone the traffic police on duty to obtain updates of the overall state of affairs. Occasionally there are "chitchats" about politics and current events. The latter programme has also covered services such as legal advice, reports on missing cars, requests for car repairs, and other issues from voicing grievances to concerned authorities, and to putting people on alert about all kinds of urban perils. The programme is also an interesting case of people's participation in cooperation with the private sector (a commercial bank) and the authority (Department of Mental Health, Ministry of Public Health).

In short, both programmes act as informative companions to road users. Given the snare of the traffic, they help alleviate the common plight of Bangkokians and commuters. They are made use of perhaps more widely than many other forms of participation. Taxi drivers could well verify this point. In view of a vast scale of operation and tremendous constraints, these radio programmes are extremely practical and economical. Most importantly, they are carried out by means of participation.

With this perspective in view and being encouraged by favourable outcomes of participatory urban development processes elsewhere, a pilot project was conceived for Bangkok to implement a people's planning approach to traffic and transport management. In practice it is an application of a participatory approach aiming at the formulation of comprehensive policies on urban development with transport problems as their focus. Two major considerations which have been kept in mind during the implementation of the process from its inception in 1998 till its completion in 2001 were (i) through people's participation, good governance of the city administration could be better realized, and (ii) sustainability criteria were to be central in policy formulation on urban and transport development. The former is about the organizational dimension and that of people's contribution: it is concerned with the question of how best to muster organizational and people's efforts in completing designated tasks. The latter is the technical dimension: it is concerned with the tasks to be addressed and the means by which they are to be accomplished.

With these considerations in mind, this document aims to present two corresponding action plans, namely, "Proposals for development of institutions and of people's functional groups" in Part I and "Proposals for actions to alleviate traffic/transport problems" in Part II. In pursuance of the aim, the document is accordingly divided into two parts. Part I has two main categories of action plans: **Institutional development** and **Support to People's Initiatives in Development**. Part II has **twelve action plans**. Under each category and each title, the format of presentation is conceptually arranged with the present conditions, problems and issues at the beginning, followed by the ways and means to achieve the desired outcome. Additionally, there are items on suggested readings and stakeholders' references.

Prior to their presentation, however, a background to the project area and a brief description of the elements of the planning process pursued by the pilot project are given.

The Rattanakosin Pilot Project

In line with its rationale, this pilot project adopted a participatory approach as its flag. For practical reasons a city area of a viable size was chosen. The area is known as the

Rattanakosin Area. Correspondingly the project was formally called "Sustainable Traffic and Transportation Development-Rattanakosin Pilot Project", or 'Rattanakosin Project' for the sake of brevity.

The area was chosen for its spatial significance in many ways. Though each particular place is unique in its own way, the uniqueness of the Rattanakosin Area is perhaps much more pronounced than many others. For some it is regarded as the symbolic heart of the city and even of the country. It is the *Alstadt* of Bangkok, retaining the character of the dynastic capital. Physically it houses prominent buildings associated with the royalty such as old palaces, the compound of the old royal court, the royal temple, etc. Government offices since the time of their conception are concentrated in the area. The business centre of the city once originated from here. Socially there are communities of long standing (Sam Phreangs, Klong Kuu Maung Derm and Banglamphu, to name only a few), and a large number of educational establishments and places of worship from various religions. Culturally vibrant activities of a diverse nature take place both on a regular and an occasional basis. Performances and shows are staged in the National Theatre or in Thammasat University's Auditorium as well as outdoors. Religious functions, celebrations of important days are held here on a grand scale. It also has the image of being the major site of political expression. It contains the vast field *Sanam Luang*, which has assumed a role as a multi-function space, ranging from mundane activities such as folk kite festivals to sacred ones including royal funerals. The ground also functions as an informal major bus terminal, and of late, as a sleeping site for homeless people. In short, the Rattanakosin Area as the spatial expressions of administrative, cultural, religious, political and utilitarian functions has long been appreciated.

In terms of urban transport, the Area has become a thoroughfare between the eastern and western parts of Bangkok since the construction of Pinklao Bridge in 1973. This function leads to heavy congestion in the Area during rush hours. Congestion is further compounded by traffic with trip ends generated by government and commercial offices as well as schools that attract students whose parents have sufficient means to transport them by car. In addition to commuters' vehicles, there are public bus terminals and the growth of tourism has required the Area to accommodate a large number of tourist buses visiting the historic and religious sites. Parking space is also under intense pressure from increasing demand. Being an old part of the city, it is densely populated; many roads are narrow and cannot be expanded. High-rise buildings are also not allowed due to the special cultural/historical status of the Area.

The special status of the Area was initially assumed under a special ordinance in 1978. The bicentennial celebration of Bangkok in 1982, the events of which were concentrated in the Area, established its monumental significance in the realm of public awareness. With some modifications from previous working groups, the first and current Rattanakosin Committee was formed in 1996. Considering the special status of the Area and based on the needs for conservation and for better urban and land use planning the Committee has developed a master plan. Notwithstanding its relatively small area of 5.84 sq km within Bangkok Metropolis, the Area has acquired prominent administrative and symbolic urban significance.

An area with all these special characteristics makes it a place of great interest and was therefore chosen for the pilot project. A brief description on the participatory planning process followed by the project is presented next.

The Planning and Policy Development Process

A direct and interactive involvement of the three main "actors" in policy development and plan preparation forms the essence of the process pursued. These three actors are politicians, civil servants/professionals and the public at large, and are collectively termed as stakeholders. The open involvement of the stakeholders in the process was achieved through:

- Identification of representative key stakeholders who are likely to have a view on transportation problems and issues in the pilot project area;

- A personal letter to key stakeholders from the Governor stating the importance which he places on the stakeholder's views;

- Personal interviews by core project team members of the key stakeholders;

- Documentation, in a structured manner, of all statements made by key stakeholders. This documentation known as "Anthology" was publicly available and while the identity of stakeholders was not revealed, individuals could read the statements which they made, the views they expressed and the solutions they proposed;

- Further analysing the "Anthology" of stakeholders' views with a "Problem and Cause Analysis". In this phase, the problems, symptoms and root causes were identified and their interrelationships mapped out in a series of large diagrams;

- Convening Expert Group Meetings, which included key stakeholders and technical experts, during both the "Anthology" and "Problem and Cause Analysis";

- Consultation with stakeholders at workshops for refinements of the initial outcomes;

- Developing action plans based on the outcomes of the previous stages.

The process followed in preparing the action plans is depicted in figure 1. The direct involvement of stakeholders (especially the public at large) commenced during the interview stage, when six questions were asked concerning identification of problems and their root causes, their vision of the future and the ways in which he or she could directly contribute to that vision. This was followed through in a synthesis phase where stakeholders' views were directly incorporated in the formulation of the vision and strategy for sustainable transport as well as the development of draft action plans designed to move towards the goals specified in the vision and strategy. Stakeholders were further involved in these activities through Expert Group Meetings and a series of workshops in which they directly participated through organized groups to view, fill in the missing parts and deliberate on the formulation of action plans.

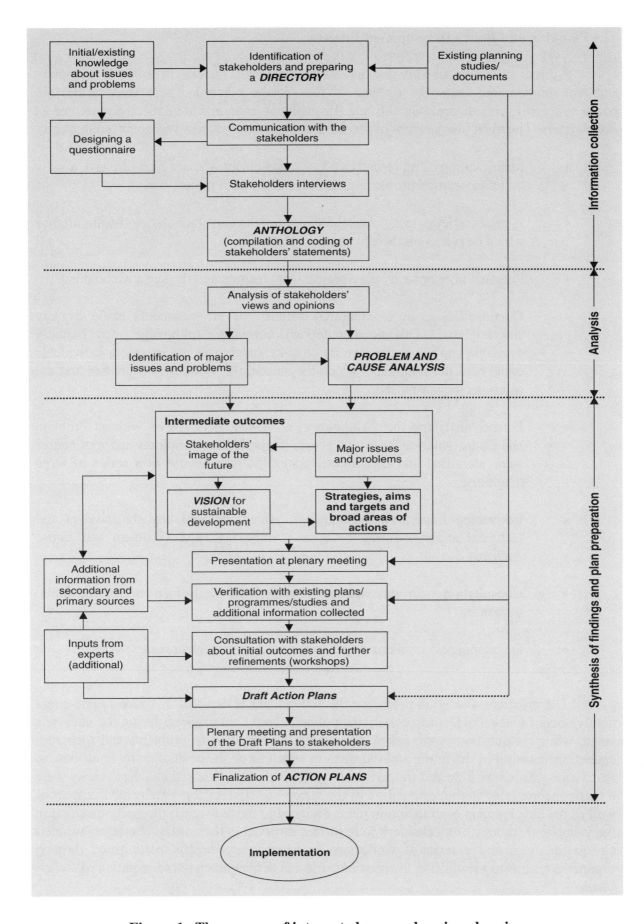

Figure 1. The process of integrated comprehensive planning

The approach in the pilot project essentially inverts the traditional approach, going first to the principal stakeholders and asking their views on the problems, the causes of the problems, the strategic goals and the means by which that can be achieved. The outcomes from the project are extremely rich in information and suggestions. They have been through the process of analysis and synthesis, and eventually ordered into the framework of action plans. As stated above the plans are broadly classified into two major categories of recommendations/proposed actions. Hereafter, the action plans under Part I and II are to follow accordingly.

PART I

**Proposals for Development of
Institutions and Support to People's Initiatives
in Development**

INTRODUCTION

Participatory approaches entail a mode of working interactively between the bureaucracy and the public. Though there is no single specific definition, a general agreement revolves around the idea of creating opportunities for people to share ideas, knowledge, and resources with the authorities to realize a common task. Theoretically speaking, inputs contributed by the people should cover all stages of a process from the beginning to the end. This requires an active involvement in design, implementation, management, and evaluation of programmes and projects, as well as ongoing activities such as maintenance.

However, given the nature of works, the type of involvement also needs to be taken into account. Two broad degrees of involvement can be qualified. In the basic form, the degree of involvement is generally low and the interaction between the authorities and the public takes place rather in an *ad hoc* fashion. In a more advanced form, the degree of involvement is high, and can be conceptualised as a partnership between the authorities and the members of public.

The basic types can take the form of primary and consultative participation. When translated into practice, they can range from simple types such as collection of information through questionnaire surveys, round table discussions, public meetings, etc., to more sophisticated varieties such as regular joint meetings and workshops. The highly developed types involve functional and interactive forms of participation. They involve cooperation between the authorities and the public that is much closer than in the basic type. Metaphorically speaking, it is like the activities of rowing and steering a boat together.

Different types of participation are appropriate to different organizational levels. A face-to-face working environment is possible only in a small-scale setting, such as at the community level. This is the level where the highly developed forms of participation or partnerships could be achievable. Whereas at the other end of the scale, the elementary forms of participation are more applicable. Nevertheless, at all levels, participation contains good governance as the key. Hence the emphasis is on good governance, which conceptually refers to four vital areas of endeavour, namely, efficiency, effectiveness, accountability and transparency. Practically, its purpose is to ensure that an organization's services are at the full disposal of the public.

Within an institutional framework, the building of public awareness is a complement to participation. Awareness creation is not confined within any particular institution: it is based on the crucial issues of public interest concerning urban problems in general. It often evolves around the actions of advocacy, and the making of public platforms. Its perspective is therefore proactive; and occasionally it may take the form of a review of urban policies.

To obtain the benefits of people's participation in urban development, action plans can be formulated in two directions, namely, (a) people's participation in institutions and (b) institutional participation in people's activities. The former direction (a) takes the institutions as given; the people takinging part in their functions. To phrase it in another way, from the perspective of the authorities, it is to institutionalise people's participation within the formal structure of an organization. As to the latter direction (b), the core is the people, whereas the authorities are peripheral. Civic groups or people's functional groups are the entities with which the organizations are to cooperate as supporting actors or facilitators.

The action plans contained in this section of the report for (a) are presented under the umbrella **institutional development**, and the action plans for (b) are presented under **support to people's initiatives in development**. They serve to realize different objectives in different contexts. These action plans are designed to realize people's potentials in urban development and management. This could be achieved through good governance within the sphere of city administration on the one hand, and promoting people's initiatives in the public sphere on the other.

As to the organizations designed for people to participate, the sizes and the structures vary from one authority to another. The size can be from as large as that of Bangkok Metropolitan Administration (BMA) with two headquarters, 50 district offices, a few water treatment plants, a few large-size hospitals, a large number of schools covering the whole area of Bangkok Metropolis, etc., to a modest organization with a single central office located in a building like the Office of the Commission for the Management of Land Traffic (OCMLT). Service-wise, urban services are rendered by different organizations and their respective organizational configurations have their own histories and rationales. For instances, the Metropolitan Water Works Authority has one centralized office similar to the Telephone Organization of Thailand, but the latter provides services nationwide. The Metropolitan Electricity Authority on the other hand has its headquarters and 14 branch offices to cover some adjacent areas to Bangkok as well. If focusing on services, non-residents of Bangkok could be easily perplexed. Transportation, education and healthcare, not to say of urban development in general, are administered by a large number of public sector organizations and also by the private sector.

There have long been persistent arguments that in order to provide better services to the urban population, all services, which are now spread out to various authorities, in the metropolitan area of Bangkok, should be unified under a single organization, i.e., BMA. The issues are much too complex for a small-scale project like the present one to consider. Besides, the main task of this project is to address the question of how participatory approaches could be further advanced in urban development rather than to tackle the problems of urban administration in general.

Here, participation related to the functions of BMA has been singled out and outlined for two reasons. First, it is the most important authority for the population in Bangkok. Second, some forms of participation have already been functioning in the system, which could purposefully be enhanced. At present participation is principally through elected representatives at the city and district levels. There are, however, other possibilities of participation that could be encouraged, introduced, and institutionalised in the long run.

The following action plans are principally based on the ideas and proposals from stakeholders' interviews and community workshops. Together with some inputs from expert meetings and seminars with concerned agencies, they were formulated and submitted for review by the original proponents and deliberation by the policy makers. However, they should not to be regarded as panacea, but considered as broad options to be judiciously and incrementally chosen from.

Each action plan draws the idea from the concept of participatory approaches for its presentation. With a modification of the well-practiced SWOT method in mind (Collective consideration on Strength, Weakness, Opportunities, Threats), each proposal of the action plan is composed of 8 components, namely, (i) background and current situation; (ii) strengths of the present situation; (iii) its weaknesses; (iv) issues and major problems; (v) directions of desirable change and aims; (vi) proposed actions, (vii) further studies, and (viii) stakeholders' references.

Institutional Development

INTRODUCTION

Bangkok Metropolitan Administration (BMA) as the main and most prominent organization for the city has travelled along the road of institutional development for a long time. Within the existing mandate of the organization, one can hardly conceive the possibility for new units for novel functions to be added onto its present organizational structure, a diagram of which is presented in figure 2. BMA basically has the essential and necessary functions that a modern organization for urban services should have. The purpose of introducing people's participation is to complement and enhance those functions of the organization.

In order to accomplish more profoundly its mandates, BMA, as any other public organization, is required to inspire an ever-higher degree of administrative governance. Administrative governance is a sub-set of governance indicating "a system of policy implementation carried out through an efficient, independent, accountable and open public sector."[6] It is theoretically conceived and empirically convincing that the inspiration can be better achieved, inter alia, by means of people's participation. Applied to BMA, people's participation could be incorporated into the organization from the central to the sub-district levels, with each level institutionalising a different form of participation to realize different objectives. Against this rationale the proposed action plan aims to achieve cooperation and partnerships between BMA and the communities.

I. BACKGROUND AND CURRENT SITUATION

There is a wide gap between the actual number of people living in Bangkok and that of those registered as residents. By a conservative estimate, the daytime population is well over 10 millions. But the latest publication of the statistical profile of BMA (1999) shows the number of registered residents as 5,647,799 in total. A proportion of the adult population occasionally, albeit regularly, go to the polls to cast their votes for their representatives. The popularity of election, however, dwindles from the gubernatorial to the city and the district levels. The election is the main system through which people can participate in the city administration.

Outside of the election seasons the contact between BMA public officials and the public concerning planning and policy formulation or day-to-day management of urban services is tenuous. As a general rule, BMA takes the role of service provider and the public are assumed to be satisfied as the recipients.

However, there have been attempts to involve the communities into the working of BMA at the district and sub-district levels. A number of resident groups in Rattanakosin Area have been organized into officially recognized communities. Taking Pranakorn District, a major administrative unit in the Area, as an illustration, there are 21 such communities. Each of these spatial communities sets up a community representative organization (CRO) comprising around 15 committee members representing around 280-300 households, or 1,500-1,700 people (which can go up to 2,000). Out of the rank and file members, 20-30 active and vocal people usually attend meetings and maintain contacts with officials.

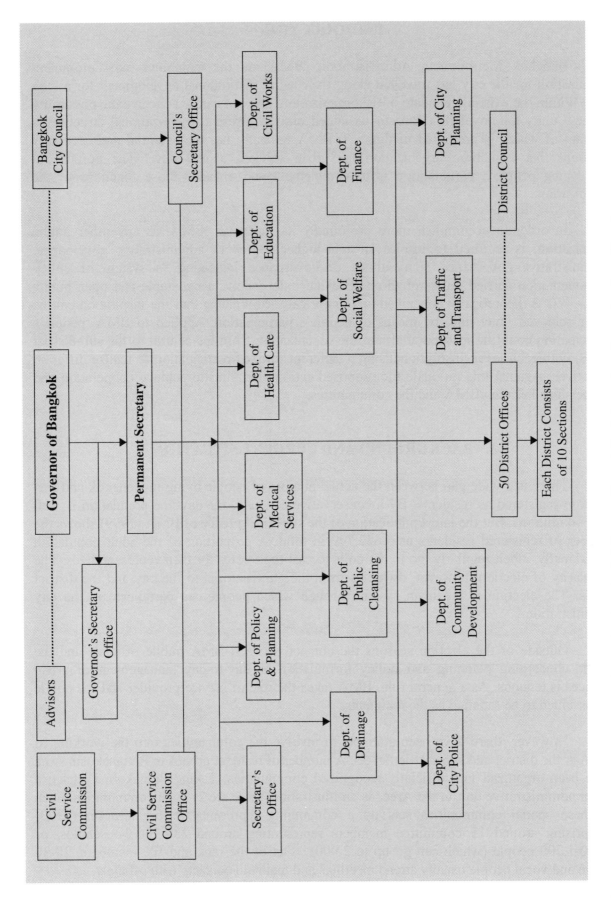

Figure 2. Bangkok Metropolitan Administration Organization Chart

In addition to participation by means of electoral representation through popular voting, therefore, there are also some other kinds of limited participatory activities in BMA. The present arrangements for participation, however, fall short of people's expectations and of present-day development requirements. The overall situation is also indicative of a number of predicaments in the city's administration; (i) a large number of people residing in Bangkok are disenfranchised due to the residential registration system; (ii) the importance of the BMA offices is concentrated at the centre, and diluted as the work units get down to the grass-root level; and (iii) the people, cannot make much contribution in the city's development and management of services due to lack of close interaction with the authority.

II. STRENGTHS OF THE PRESENT SITUATION

The potentials of the people are, as it were, omnipresent. These potentials can be turned into major resources, which can contribute to improving the socio-economic and physical environment of the city. This has been demonstrated by a number of successful activities in Bangkok in the recent years. The communities on *Pra Arthit Rd.,* in the course of working with some NGOs and the university nearby, came to realize that a busy road could be turned into a lively environment, not ridden by vehicles but by strolling people. The rehabilitation of an old fort into a promenade/park was impressively carried out by the authorities with strong support from the community. The community members are now not merely users, but jointly taking care of it as well. The concept of *Fussgangerzones* and the maintenance of parks have proven also to be popular novel ideas which could be carried out only with people's participation.

Less visible are ubiquitous, though small, activities run by various communities. Those activities have been going on either with some assistance from the official funding or very often carried out independently by the community's own meagre resources. Sports activities, greening of the areas, and cleaning of places, security surveillances, parking arrangement, etc. are but only a few examples of people's initiatives, that have been undertaken in some parts of Bangkok.

There are many more proposals which can be implemented if the authorities agree. For example, in the matters of local-level traffic management, and small repairs and maintenance works, there can be found many potential volunteers. The volunteers could help monitor the traffic flow in small *soi* (lanes), they could also act as traffic wardens in cooperation with the traffic police. With supplies from BMA, people with basic building skills can deal with the repairs of broken manhole covers, maintenance of road surface and street furniture, disentanglement of wires with tree branches, painting of houses and communal areas, etc.

The community organizers also have ways and tact to manage problems. A good example is how to call for a meeting. If done in an official manner, only a few would turn up. "We must make a call for "*Sangsan*" (to join together merrily)". Many people find it difficult and have not much time to spare for the community, let alone for the authority, unless they could enjoy the occasion as well. The timing for activities is also very important. They must not necessarily be during office hours, or on dates to suit the officials.

People's interests in their communities have been well reflected in extensive news coverage of BMA activities in various mass media. A number of daily newspapers, radio and television stations always devote space and time to the city affairs. That is to say people persistently follow, and are being fed with information on how their problems and wishes are addressed. This testifies to the fact that the people have a keen interest in participation and the situation is unlike in some other cities where people's apathy towards participation prevents institutionalisation of participatory approaches.

III. WEAKNESSES OF THE SITUATION

Though it can be said that the CRO is recognized by the authority, it is only as far as the working relationship between the public and BMA is concerned. The CRO is intrinsically an informal entity, and has no statutory status. It may be argued that the status itself may not entail any problem, as long as the group could work for communities. But without a legal standing, it is not always possible to carry out activities that an active organization would have liked to have done. The CRO is, for example, not entitled to enter into contracts, solicit funding, take on liabilities under its name, etc. In practice the CRO is usually regarded as an appendage of the authority. Theoretically, all of its architectural, engineering and public works tasks are to be done by BMA, however by certain agreements some elementary works can be delegated to the CRO.

According to the current arrangements, the district authority of the BMA is to hold meetings with the CRO on a monthly basis. However, with their other workloads, the meetings are rather infrequent. The meetings are actually held around 4-5 times in a year. The call for meetings is within the prerogative of the authority. In principle the communities can determine the agenda as well. But more commonly, the meetings turn out to be a platform of the authority to explain plans and official initiatives for the communities.

Each community is entitled to a monthly budgetary allocation of 2,000 baht. In compliance with the official rules, the community has to go through the process from submitting a proposal, getting approval, … and eventually may get the payment. The budget allocation process for the community is theoretically sensible, and practically useful, but it comes with certain problems. For example, the procedure is cumbersome, and it takes a long time to get the money. Often the community members need to spend in advance from their own pockets; the amount is pitiful and not always worth taking the trouble; in some cases the goods supplied through the official channel are low both in quantity and in quality; and sometimes the money can become a divisive factor within the community.

In each community there are people usually willing to contribute their time, skills and physical efforts for the sake of a common good. To realise more fully and to sustain their contributions the work environment needs to be sufficiently encouraging. But sometimes they feel undervalued or even discouraged. Additionally, real difficulties in work implementation often lie with certain kinds of work requiring substantial expenses, which cannot be met out of the present petty monthly allocation.

IV. MAJOR ISSUES AND PROBLEMS

BMA, similar to many other municipal organizations in Asia, has certain key characteristics. Two of them are the centralized organizational structure, and the style of bureaucratic management. These two characteristics have complex interrelationships and generally one reinforces the other. They affect not only work efficiency, but they are also not conducive to the promotion or fostering of public participation.

The overall mode of operation of BMA, like all other state organizations, must conform to the rules and regulations of the Office of the Civil Service Commission. The budget allocation and utilization are subject to the management of the Ministry of Finance. There are many other organizations with which BMA has to work. All these make the working of BMA an extremely complex undertaking both on a daily as well as on an annual basis. The basis for participatory urban development essentially is to find room for people's participation in the self-contained organization of BMA.

Given the self-contained structure of the organization, BMA functions following its own accord. Though juristically it is under the Ministry of Interior, practically it has a great deal of independence. People's participation, by means of popular election, is institutionalised in three bodies, namely, the Governorship, the Bangkok Metropolitan Council, and the District Councils. Their influences and significance are in the descending order. The most important office is, as a matter of course, that of the governor. He gives directions and instructions to the Permanent Secretary of the BMA for implementation. The Secretary, who is pivotal to all the functionaries of BMA, in turn gives instructions to the 14 Departments as well as to the 50 District offices directly under him.

The Bangkok Metropolitan Council comprises 60 elected representatives, one from each district but districts with large populations have two members. One of the major roles of the Council is to approve the annual budget of the BMA. Each district has a district council consisting of seven elected councillors. The District Council has an advisory role at the district level.

The brief outline given above is merely to convey the idea that the three bodies typify the system of representative democracy. The relationship between the elected and the electors is loosely outlined on an *ad hoc* basis. The elected representatives, in the name of their electors, use their own discretion in the decision making process, or in giving advice (in the case of the district councillors). "The will of the people" is periodically honoured, and listened to particularly during the election campaign period. For most people, the election is the main and only means for participation in the decision-making process involving the affairs of the city.

Admittedly this simple sketch cannot do justice to an organization with the complexities and subtleties of the machineries such as that of BMA. Hopefully it portrays the two distinctive characteristics of BMA, namely, a highly centralized organization on the one hand, and a kind of representative democracy at work on the other.

V. DIRECTION OF DESIRABLE CHANGE AND ITS AIMS

The policies from the top are generally based on a forward-looking perspective with conservative assumptions. Ideally, a policy is formulated in response to people's problems, current or some potential problems of the future. In reality, however, noble as they may be, they may not well respond to real needs. Even well intended policies do not necessarily answer practical constraints, particularly in terms of the local context. The issue, therefore, is the problem in the process of policy formulation. Inputs from the people are not always included and generally marginalized.

The account so far generally corresponds to the view from the ground, i.e., at the implementation stage. Prior to this stage the upper levels of conduct have significant influences on the work environment at the ground level. Therefore examining, how the overall situation is addressed, and how a particular policy regarding certain problems is formulated is also very crucial. Policy formulation at the top level, which is usually not within the realm of people's participation, is not to be left out of consideration.

The current limited scope and low degree of participation in the city's development administration is due primarily to the centralized organizational characteristics of BMA, and lack of a variety of institutional mechanisms to participate. It is therefore logical to strive towards two aims, namely, decentralization and participatory democracy. The former will pave the ways for the latter, and vice versa.

Obviously it is not possible for the people to participate directly in a meaningful way in a large organization. For a greater opportunity for people to participate, a viable size of work-setting is necessary. Thereby, decentralization becomes a key concept. The office at the grass-root level, the sub-district or lower, could well be more accessible to the people at large. Necessary also is the delegation of tasks, together with necessary budget allocation. The office at each level should not be meant primarily to carry out tasks given from the higher offices. It should be able to act as a conduit for issues, problems and policy related proposals to be transmitted to higher offices. It should also be in a position to determine its own priorities and deliver services in a way that best reflects local needs and circumstances and in an effective and efficient manner.

It has now been duly recognized by the urban governance actors from different parts of the world that the growing urban economic, social and environmental problems can effectively be addressed only through the creativity and motivation of citizens at the local level. Without support of citizens, the traditional bureaucratic management of urban affairs is no longer sufficient to handle the complexity of today's problems. The primary role of local governments is, therefore, to empower citizens to meet these challenges. This would also be in line with the aspirations of the people in a society where the values of democracy are widely shared.

If local people are involved in local planning, knowledge about local conditions and problems are readily available. Costly and time-consuming data gathering is not always needed. Their ideas could be utilized, and hence solutions became easily acceptable to all. The community potentialities can be actualised, if a working rapport between the authority and the community could be ensued. Moreover, the course of people's participation could also automatically serve as the process of conflict resolution between various groups of a community that may like to pursue different sets of goals.

The concepts of decentralization and people's participation are neither alien to society in general nor to the bureaucracy in particular. On the contrary, they are in line with the general aspirations of the people of Thailand. Section 78 of the Constitution (1997) states as follows: "The State shall decentralize powers to localities for the purpose of independence and self-determination of local affairs, develop local economies, public utilities and facilities systems and information infrastructure in the locality thoroughly and equally throughout the country…" Concerning people's participation, Section 76 previously mentioned states that people's participation is to be promoted in matters such as policy formulation and political decision-making. In simple terms, as provided in these two sections on local governance the constitution recognizes, "…people have the right to govern and administer their hometowns and make decisions on local affairs, including development projects. The State must therefore render such authority to local administrations."[7] Therefore, as the basic principles have already been laid down, it is now a matter of translating them into practice.

The direction of change at the national level and other levels of local government could well provide a supportive environment for desirable change within BMA. Different agencies may have different ways to translate the two principles into action. But for a genuine change, both of people's participation and decentralization need to go hand in hand.

Decentralization may not be just limited to devolution of power within the organization itself. The heart of the matter is that the structure is to be modified and/or reformed to accommodate a greater degree of popular participation. To accomplish this aim, it is necessary to apply the principle to every echelon, from the top to the district and to lower levels.

VI. PROPOSED ACTIONS

A. Decentralization

1. Making the sub-district or *Khaeng* an administrative unit

Given the size and the scope of activities, the district is a large entity responsible for a large population (on average the number of registered residents per district is more than 100,000 people). The district, being equivalent to the *Amphoe* in the rural area, is the lowest administrative tier of BMA. *Khaeng* or sub-district, a spatial unit under the district, has no legal status, nor an administrative unit in its own right. Compared to the local government system in the rural areas, it is ironical that Bangkok is less advanced than the rest of Thailand. Outside urban Bangkok there exists an officially recognized unit below the district level. It has even a self-governing body, the well-known Tambon Administrative Organization (TAO).

The creation of the *Khaeng* as an administrative unit below the district level would be a rational step to keep urban local government reform in line with the ongoing changes in reorganization of the local government system in rural areas. It could take TAO as a possible replica, (it could even be named "Khaeng Administrative Organization – KAO") with certain budget allocation and be run by a body of elected representatives. Similar to TAO, it could be in charge of functions related to local affairs, i.e. the management of matters such as:

- Public health (mosquito sprays, control of stray dogs, health cards, and communal cold drinking water);
- Municipal services (garbage collection, street cleaning, etc.);
- Neighbourhood access road maintenance;
- Sports and recreational activities;
- Plantation and streetscaping;
- Other matters of community concerns.

Many stakeholders held the view that authorities should provide support to communities to organize their own affairs. The creation of the *Khaeng* could enable them to do so.

2. Extension of the administrative autonomy of the District Office

With the creation of a *Khaeng* Administrative Organization as an administrative unit, the district office could then have two main responsibilities, namely, to serve as the coordinating office for the KAOs within its boundary, and to operate as the self-functioning unit regarding the matters of district's concern. As to the first responsibility it could, upon request, help organize meetings, address issues that cut across boundaries of more than one KAO, as well as work on issues of common concern for KAOs. In order to realize economies of scale, and address "externalities" the district office would have comparative advantage in material procurements and in tasks beyond the confine of a particular *Khaeng*.

After an agreed division of responsibility with the KAOs, the district office could carry out similar types of works. But more importantly, it is a view held by many stakeholder that the district office should be given greater autonomy. Since different districts have their own peculiarities, each district office would need to have plans and programmes of its own, provided they were compatible with the overall plan and the general policy direction of BMA. (Greening the area, for example, could be better achieved with local innovations and operation - the kinds of trees need not be the same all over Bangkok.)

The step to a greater autonomy would not necessarily mean drastic changes. The communities entertain moderate wishes, requesting the district chiefs to be responsive to the community needs. For example, there has not been any demand to hold an extra election at the district level. (In fact, the question "how about the idea that the district chief is not an appointed position, but an elected official similar to the BMA governor?" always received a negative answer). The district chief can be anyone. It does not matter how he/she is appointed, so long as the person understands (meaning "is sympathetic to") the community's needs.

The two essential components of greater autonomy are related to finance and functions. A district office could be entitled to a direct budget allocation related to its own work plans, which would have to be approved by the governor and the Bangkok Metropolitan Council. The question of revenue collection, however, can be considered in the long run. As to the functions at the district level, they need to be considered in relation to the new assignments of the KAO and of the Departments at the central level. But certainly more functions than at present can be delegated at the district level. The main point is that the execution of its functions could be carried out by decisions at the district level.

3. Modification of the roles of the Central Office

As the district offices could be given greater roles in taking initiatives and of operation, the roles of the Departments at the centre could also be modified. For example, the roles of the fourteen departments could fall into two major categories, namely, those whose tasks cover all areas of Bangkok and those whose tasks could be done by district offices. The first group would include departments such as education, medical services, city planning, etc., whereas the second group would include public cleansing, community development, drainage and sewerage, etc.

24

The departments in the second category could be restructured from being operational units to units assuming supervisory roles. Matters concerning traffic and transportation, presently holding department status, for example, could be substantially delegated and transferred to the district offices and even the KAOs. The functions of the Department of Social Welfare are clearer. Their planning and implementation activities could be better carried out at the KAO level with the support of their respective district offices and under supervision and technical assistance from the Department at the central level.

The departments whose functions are to be delegated to the district offices could act as liaison bodies forming networks and coordinators for all district offices and even for KAOs in certain circumstances.

It is well known that fiscal autonomy is an essential parameter for administrative decentralization. Certainly there could be different ways and different levels of budgetary management. Instead of having the communities going through a rigid bureaucratic procedure, which is clearly not conducive to the community's work initiatives, the budget may be given to each community as a lump sum. The authority could of course inspect and monitor spending. As observed by a community leader "The management of funds earmarked for helping people has much of constrains, for instance the Mayazawa Fund."[8] There has been a common complaint that the communities never see the money, and the goods delivered out of the fund through the authority are much less, both in quality and quantity, than the requests from the communities.

However, communities may not always want the support in monetary form, but in the form of materials (e.g. paint so that they can do the work of painting by themselves). If the money is given to certain individuals even understood as community leaders, it could still cause conflicts within a community. But by means of people's participation the financial matters could be better managed as well.

To reiterate, actions for the reform of the organization need to be considered at all levels. The prime consideration should be on the *Khaeng* as it would be mostly associated with the communities. From the community's perspective most services required by them could be delivered by operating at the sub-district level. For the *Khaeng* to be able to do so, the higher tiers of the organization need to be supportive. As any change at one level will have direct bearings on the others, all those three levels are to be considered together. With this in view and taking the *Khaeng* as the basis, future reforms at the other levels need to be considered in a comprehensive and integrated way.

B. People's participation

One of the principle functions of decentralization is to ensure that services provided by the government more adequately reflect the needs of local people through the facilitation of people's participation. Here, participation means contributing to development, benefiting from development and taking part in decision-making about development, which could be realized through activities facilitated by authorities as well as activities initiated or generated by the people themselves. Participation should be understood as a process in which all concerned parties and the affected people are involved in decision-making about development works and delivery of public goods and services. People's involvement could be realized in many ways and by different methods. However, they are to be designed and made compatible with the characteristics of the task to be accomplished, and of the culture being practiced and to be cultivated.

People's participation in urban development and management can be practiced in reality in different forms at different levels and its nature could also vary by purpose. The nature and form of participation much depend on three major factors, i.e. mission, organizational structure and spatial level. The mission factor specifies 'what needs to be done' or defines a job to be accomplished, whereas the organizational factor provides the framework for conducting participation, and the spatial level is the geographical extent to which the previous two factors are related. These factors are to be considered in conjunction with the basic principles laid down in state policies and legal instruments, and practicalities such as the nature of the issue, population size, geographical coverage and various constraints.

Taking the existing organizational framework as a point of departure, people's participation can be practiced at three levels, i.e. the city, the district and the sub-district level. Participation at these levels could have different missions and different objectives to achieve. Consequently, the nature and form of participation would vary at these three levels. Whatever may be the chosen method and form of participation, they have common denominators i.e., all methods and forms are to heed the principle of "engaging affected people and concerned people in open dialogue through which a range of views and concerns can be expressed in order to inform decision-making and help in creating mutual understanding despite different interests."[1] More details on nature, form and techniques of participation at the city, the district and the sub-district level are provided next.

City level

At the city level, the mission primarily relates to overall planning and policy development and thereby very broad in scope, spatially extensive, and organizationally wholesome. At this level, participation would not be direct but could be mediated through the mass media, the Internet and by articulated advocacy groups. By making necessary information available to the public at large, the authority in consultation with the advocacy groups could develop and share a collective vision about the city, and eventually set the goals and priorities. The broad objective of participation was to achieve a common understanding and build general consensus regarding strategic issues at the city level. This form of participation can be called "consultative participation".

The advocacy groups could be selected from a broad spectrum of the urban society representing, for example, citizens groups, professional bodies, civil society, NGOs, business associations, ethno-religious groups, voluntary foundations, slum residents groups, senior citizens groups, women's platforms, etc. The representatives, with a popular approval of some kind, may form people's committees. The committees, sharing information with authorities, were to develop a vision, identify issues, define problems and deliberate on available broad policy options for their solutions. The power in decision-making would be limited. Nevertheless, suggestions and advice by committees could have bearing on final decisions. In addition to contribution in policy formulation through their advocacy roles, the

---

[1]   A draft on Public Participation in Environmental Aspects in ASEM Countries by Finnish Environmental Institute and Thailand Environmental Institute, 2001, (publication: forthcoming).

groups could also help clarify problematic issues to the general public and mobilise popular support with respect to hard policy choices.

District level

The mission at the district level could relate to both planning and implementation. Broad tasks to be performed are by and large well stipulated by the strategic planning framework at the city level, whereas the methods of participation are open. The area of coverage is still wide but within the limits of a manageable size by means of indirect representation through focus groups. Focus groups could form a part of both planning and implementation task force at the district level. This form of participation can be called" functional participation".

Functional participation would be more direct and the relationship between authority and the people would be towards developing partnerships. People involved in participation may be recruited from different active groups. They could come from, for example, socially committed groups, civic groups, or informal groups such as people who meet on a regular basis at parks or temples, or mosques. It is important to note here that civil society organizations could play a crucial role in fostering participation, building trust, articulating local interests and views, and exploiting local opportunities.

The participation may largely be concerned with problem identification and specific policy formulation from which general guidelines for actions could be drawn. In the context of implementation, once policies and their implications are clarified, and given that goals and the general directions were already established, people's committees could help define a range of decision options. Together with permanent officials they could jointly put efforts for setting priorities and agreed procedures for actions to be taken.

The committee could also extend their help to the district office to make it more friendly towards people coming to seek assistance. As felt by some of the stakeholders "We find the district office rather overwhelming." There could be certain representatives working (mobile, or otherwise) to help those who come to the office for some purpose.

Sub-District Level

At the sub-district level, which would be closest to the common people, the mission primarily relates to implementation of development activities and delivery of municipal services at the community level. The participation at this level could of direct form and interactive in nature through substantive involvement of the rank and file people within a confined geographical limit in implementation of projects, programmes or management of neighbourhoods. Valuable ideas, which the locals are in possession through their experience, could contribute to the solution of physical, social and environmental problems at the micro level. Pursuing local initiatives and supporting constant interaction between officials and local residents could be the focus of participation at this level. The mechanism of participation could be in the form of joint working committees or other suitable means at the street or community level. This form of direct participation can be called "interactive participation".

This level is yet to benefit from the institutional infrastructure. With the long-term aim of establishing sub-district offices, some kind of joint coordination committees could be formed at this stage. Their functions could vary from addressing grievances to making facilities, both physical and institutional, more accessible to the people living in the community. The committees could make direct contributions as well as help the functionaries achieve better performance, in terms of designing and implementation of development projects, and provision and management of urban services.

CONCLUSIONS

Participation is essential in people's lives. By participation their voices are heard and they are empowered; they gain recognition, respect and dignity; they can decide how best to utilize the assets for their common benefit. Our experience suggests that all stakeholders including the poor, women, people with special needs, and the community be involved in a transparent decision-making process to seek inter-disciplinary solutions to urban problems. Responsive planning and dialogue between various groups that have conflicts of interest can generate solutions, which may be generally acceptable to all. To ensure people's participation, a fundamental institutional change in the planning and decision-making process is required. Decentralization of the planning process and devolution of power at the local/community levels are essential to institutionalize participation in a meaningful way. These in turn would require organizational reform, social mobilization of the community and marginal groups, and development programmes with a focus on locally planned and managed development and supporting the local needs and initiatives taken by the people themselves.

SUGGESTED READINGS

As the themes, decentralization, participatory approaches and partnership with community, underlying the action plan are among the critical contemporary issues, related publications are numerous in number. The body of current literature on the subject matter is extremely rich with information on practical experiences about decentralization and people's participation in the affairs of urban local governments and delivery of municipal services through partnerships with the private sector and nongovernmental organizations from different parts of the world. Leaving those academic in outlook, some selected practical-oriented works elsewhere could prove to be useful reference. (Full references are provided in the bibliography at the end of this report.)

1) *India: The Challenge of Urban Governance* addresses, inter alia, the questions of institutional aspects of urban governance, participation and urban governance, and fiscal innovations. The issues addressed in the book are directly relevant to the action plan, and more importantly they are based on problems and experiences very much akin to cities in developing countries. The book provides food for thought, giving stimulating perspectives on which further actions could be based.

2) *Asian Cities in the 21st Century, vol 4: Partnerships for Better Municipal Management* attempts to offer new ways to tackle both new and old problems facing cities in a number of countries in Asia, including Thailand. They are not merely ideas desirable for implementation, but based on lessons learned

from direct experiences in improving governance and delivery of municipal services through partnerships with the private sector and nongovernmental organizations. The book gives a wide range of good practices, which could be regarded as models for one's own policy formulation.

3) *Making Cities Work* is extremely rich in both information and thinking, and at the same time offers tips of recommendations, check lists, models for action plans, successful actions, etc. In its own description "This book outlines some of the practical measures that local authorities all over the world have initiated, and the policies that will help them to take this work further... the initiatives being taken range from housing and employment schemes to traffic management and public transport, ... In this work, local authorities are acting in partnership with groups in their own communities..."

4) *The City and the Grassroots* may be read more in the academic world than by practitioners. But it gives so much insight to the relationship between cities and social change. The theses, indicating the important roles of the state, of the economy, of technology and of other social parameters in shaping cities, are drawn from several case studies, current as well as historical. They could make practitioners conscious of impacts of various intervening forces. In the words of a reviewer "Required reading for planners. It is not only the finest comparative study of urban social movements available, but it also suggests the path to a new urban vision in opposition to the spatial program of the dominant class...It is a first-rate scholarly achievement." (Journal of the American Planning Association).

STAKEHOLDERS' REFERENCES

On participation in planning and decision-making:

060116   Community participation is necessary.

020701   I will cooperate with the government conservation policy of building colours on Rajadamnern Avenue as I did before.

020802   I will join with the BMA as one of the committees to develop Rajadamnern and Phra Nakorn city planning.

040402   Work plans should include forums forming public opinions before implementation, since they will be sounding boards of the communities to voice about the projects.

040402   City planning should be based on general surveys and public opinions in Rattanakosin Area and among the general public. And the city plans should be committed, not changing with different policies of the city administrators.

On partnerships in implementation:

010405   Willing to participate in every project as planner, activist, mediator, creator, presenter, and to establish a foundation to raise funds from foreign corporations and to manage human resources.

020501   BMA should ask for cooperation from building and shop owners to revitalize their buildings (old style buildings) and perhaps to share responsibilities of buying paints to redecorate them. The entertainment places should have their own zones outside Rattanakosin Area.

On transparency/ monitoring bodies/governance:

040205	Give more authority to district councils to be applied into practical policies.
060206	Develop officers to do their jobs with loyalty and concentrate on public more than personal interests.
022602	High-ranking officers should monitor the officers at work. They could be allowed to do other works after they have finished their own jobs. If the high-ranking officers were strict with the officers' works, they would not dare to escape from their works.
022704	Solve the problems of irresponsible officers.
050105	Monitor and control public lands to avoid land encroachment.
010202	Set up effective sections which have absolute authority in solving traffic and other problems.

Decentralization :

060202	Support community self-administration such as Phra Arthit community to organize its own affairs.
100105	Changes are to be made to allow higher roles for the private sector, and that the officers will control the works. Make small offices to have higher efficiency and quality.
080101	Decentralize growth and urbanization.
060307	Improve the city planning to be more suitable for each locality, and make clear zoning (including the sub-zones). The government should delegate authorities to small units to make such policies of planning.
060308	Promote development in any aspect in local areas and avoid centralization.

Support to People's Initiatives in Development

INTRODUCTION

People's interests and ideas do not necessarily coincide with the mandates and functions of authorities. They cover a wide range of issues and very often are outside the scope of BMA's works, and that of other government agencies working for Bangkok or the Rattanakosin Area. The management of transport demand, or beautification of a waterfront, conservation of historic buildings and of cultural places, problems of public safety, promotion of ethical and sustainable tourism, etc., are only a few examples of stakeholders' deep concerns. Many of these issues cannot be addressed by single organizations, but by several bodies. In reality, the real solutions could require involvement of public agencies beyond the existing charter of duties of BMA.

People's desperation to know the possibility of flooding in a province offers an interesting case study. Whether or not an area under risk was going to be flooded naturally depended on the amount of rainfall in the catchment area of the rivers flowing down into the risk area. The problem was to determine which authority was in a position to give the answer. The Meteorological Department could give a weather forecast concerning how much rain was expected to fall in the catchment area. The Royal Irrigation Department could tell the water level in the reservoirs, and how much water it was going to release downstream. The Naval Hydrographic Department knew the water level at specific stations at particular points in time. Undoubtedly information from each agency was required to answer the question. But the answer could not be obtained from any of the agencies. In particular, each of them had to refer to the information from the other two units. Eventually the question 'flooded or not flooded' was answered by the water itself!

The public are not particularly concerned with piecemeal information, but rather with the comprehensiveness of the relevant information. People's perspectives, being based on their own experiences and expectations, could differ a great deal from the authorities' views which may have been shaped by various factors, e.g., regulations, organizational histories, politics, lack of understanding about people's needs, and budgetary allocation. Public agencies are entrusted with specific duties basically to serve the people, which they may not always be in a position to carry out in the best possible way as wanted by the people. Priorities of the people could be different.

This action plan outlines how priorities can be given to people's own initiatives, and the authorities can play a supportive role to this end. To encourage and to accommodate the initiatives in question, the authorities could call for proposals from the people, as a point of departure. The proposals could be directly related to community development or for awareness building. The former is self-explanatory; the latter could be in the form of bringing issues to public consciousness, or articulating 'a state of mind': what should or should not be done.

Following this brief introduction is the exposition of each component of the action plan.

I. BACKGROUND AND CURRENT SITUATION

In the course of national development in Thailand, the state agencies have become increasingly large, some may say too large. Though the agencies are in a position to give more services to the public, the services come with high costs. To address the problem, institutional reform of the public agencies about redefining their roles and changing their organizational structure and operating practices has been on the Government's agenda for almost a decade. The ideas of "re-engineering" and of "downsizing" of the state agencies are familiar to both government officials and the public. The ideas have been translated into action in certain categories of agencies, for example, state enterprises, health care, and education.

As for those many other categories of agencies remaining intact, they have increasingly engaged private sector organizations to provide additional services and/or to complement their efforts. In the case of public transport services, the 'green buses' of different private companies and the 'sky train' of the BTS (Bangkok Transit System) and community organized solid waste management are few obvious cases in point. The trend points to the direction that society, as distinct from the state, is assuming greater direct roles in public affairs.

With the promulgation of the new law in 1985 on which BMA is structured, the current number of personnel running the organization is 87,501. The number of its functions has grown from 20 to 27 and presently to 44. They cover vast areas of urban activities ranging from the conventional functions such as road building, maintenance and traffic management, waste water treatment, drainage, building control, conservancy, city planning, maintenance of public places to less conventional functions such as, animal husbandry, sports promotion, provision and management of cemeteries and crematoriums, and also many other less conceivable functions, e.g., pawn broking business, and HIV/AIDS prevention programme.

The growth of the functions, however, has often been at the expense of basic services. There are many long-standing complaints of the residents in general and of the people from the poor quarters of the city in particular, concerning inadequacy of garbage collection, lack of anti-flooding measures, prolongation of water logging, absence of waste water pipes and sewerage system.

As previously stated, a large number of items on the stakeholders' mind do not fall into the defined functions of BMA or expertise of any body, but people themselves. Drug abuse, civic education, self-employment schemes, painting of house façades, campaign for car-free days, are few examples, which could only be dealt with by individuals or collectives, but not by official organizations.

II. STRENGTHS OF THE PRESENT SITUATION

In many parts of Bangkok, particularly in close-knit communities such as those in slum areas, self-help organizations and community-based platforms have flourished in response or in reaction to the poor service delivery system. Community programmes such as day-care centres and one-baht-a-day school programme, have been widely praised. An outstanding local innovation of garbage management, in which garbage is traded for eggs or toys, has been the talk of the town.

The community-based system utilizes local labour force, and is much more cost-effective than the conventional management system. Credit unions, small-scale savings cooperatives, land sharing schemes, construction of walkways, collective funds for housing, for example, are repeated success stories. They are common in certain parts of Bangkok, like Klong Toey and Bangkhaen, where people are presently living and were evacuated earlier from slum areas around the centre of the city. As opined by some stakeholders, "People in a community should cooperate among themselves, don't wait for BMA or the district office." And also, "In small *sois* (lanes, streets) people should take care of their own community."

It is worthy to note here that the women have played a key role in all of those success stories concerning community development through people's own initiatives. They did not only make up the core workforce, but also gave a gender perspective to urban development at the local level. "We have helped our children and husbands so much already, now a part of our lives should be devoted to our communities." "We have experience how to manage our households, why can't we manage our communities too?"

Common also is the support received from the authorities, once the communities have demonstrated their capacities to address problems through their own efforts. There are cases where in the first place residents' pledges for help did not receive favourable response. But after their initial success, the authorities showed more willingness to extend their hands. It seems that the authorities are willing to provide more assistance, when people first assist themselves. As also observed by a local resident, "If we are strong, and can well manage our communities, the district office will pay more attention, and be more helpful."

Community platforms, loosely or systematically organized, are also active in Rattanakosin Area. Tangible works in the areas of public awareness building and of establishing working entities have been achieved. The communities in the area of *Sam Phreangs* (Bamrungmuang-Fuengnakorn neighbourhood) have initiated many activities ranging from simple religious ceremonies for the enhancement of community spirit to expressing solidarity to the founding of a savings cooperative. The "Cooperative for the Rehabilitation of the Old Quarters" was formed not only for the preservation of the historic values of the venue, but also to provide a powerful leverage for greater development of the community movement.

The authority has been willing to give *Phra Sumeru Fortress Park* to the care and use of the Banglampoo network of communities, after their trust has been reassured by the community strength. Now they can have more extensive use of the park and the road adjacent to the park. The road on certain occasions has been turned into the only pedestrian street in Bangkok for three consecutive years. Civil and religious activities have been organized on a regular basis. On a daily basis, the park is very popular, and the BMA authority has been very receptive to community's suggestions.

However, there are many ideas, yet to be implemented. Some examples can be cited here: establishing an information centre about the availability and demand for different skills within a community could lead to a mutual self help community. Local people can help design footpaths and more effectively carry out the selection of trees and plants for greening the areas.

Volunteers can be recruited and trained, if necessary, from the communities for matters they are qualified to undertake, e.g., managing local traffic and parking, greening the area, helping the authorities to manage centres for children, women, elderly, disadvantaged, locate missing people, domestic water treatment, etc. These ideas are of great practical value and could be considered for putting into practice with minimal costs to the authority.

III. WEAKNESSES OF THE SITUATION

Compared to the number and size of communities in the Area, community-based working entities are few in number. Individualism rather than the community spirit is the predominant norm for urban ways of life. Similar to other parts of Bangkok and of other cities, people in the Area have tendencies to go their own ways and confine themselves within their own interests. If any task is to be performed, many people find it far easier to show their own verbal gesture than to taking part in any collective action.

More specific than the general socio-cultural environment is that community-organized activities face tremendous difficulties to sustain. Even some once well-known community organized activities, the seasonal local festivities in Wisuthkasat Sub-District for example, have now disappeared.

Over the last decade the Area has undergone a radical change. With the growth of tourism and other businesses in the Area, the plurality of interests has become more intense. "Employment promotion should be compatible with the character of the Area. Tourism-related commercial activities, such as sale of souvenir and of Thai food, tour guide business, should be encouraged but not pubs, bars or night clubs." "Relocate commercial and entertainment places out of this area." Residents generally find the growing night time businesses and tourist-related activities with disrepute as a great nuisance. "…outsiders come to this area to drink and then vomit and urinate at the temple wall or on the road." Common grounds for common interests have been under serious threats. If conflicts, latent and manifest, are not well managed, they become very divisive within and among communities.

A quotation from a renowned geographer is perhaps very apt here. "The city is the high point of human achievement, objectifying the most sophisticated knowledge in a physical landscape of extraordinary complexity, power, and splendour at the time as it brings together social forces capable of the most amazing socio-technical and political innovation. But it is also the site of squalid human failure, the lightning rod of the profoundest human discontents, and the arena of social and political conflict."[9]

Though there is a strong argument in favour of community participation, and enabling communities to respond to their own issues, diverse interests often pre-empt concerted efforts. Many initiatives have turned into failed attempts. Even in the case of successful initiations, they could be at risk in the long run. Additionally, inadequacy of financial and manpower resources are common causes of failure. In short, people's activities without strong support from both within and outside the community are likely to be unsustainable in the long run.

IV. MAJOR ISSUES AND PROBLEMS

The views of the authorities determine much of the development efforts, what is or what is not to be done. The policy orientation of the authority can therefore be either supportive or unsupportive/discouraging to people's actions. If the authorities monopolize development efforts, people's initiatives and actions would constantly face hindrances. On the contrary, if the authorities keep the soil as a fertile ground for people's initiatives, the seeds of their actions could grow well.

As to the people's side, their commitments are potentially resourceful. They are, however, not readily actualised, but need to be activated. And once they manifest themselves, the crucial question is how to *sustain* the spontaneity and vitality of the people without losing their social conscience and communal spirit.

V. DESIRABLE CHANGE AND ITS AIMS

People's participation implies a supporting or a complementary role of the people in relation to the core functioning role of the organization in charge. The concept of partnership signifies more of an equal footing between the people and the organization. Another step forward is the independent working of the people by their own initiatives and programmes. They could be in the forms of forums, associations, foundations, and the like. In such cases, the authorities could be in a supporting position. In place of people's participation, the condition is then changed to authority's participation.

Development efforts from the people are valuable not only in quantitative terms. The authorities, in spite of or because of their professionalism, have limitations. Critical comments in this respect are not hard to find. For example, "city planning agencies usually originate in the traditions of physical planning, and planners often find it exceedingly difficult to conceive of the city in terms other than this tradition."[10] or "...professionals are constrained by conventional thinking, and are prone to "inability to depart from the more traditional paradigms for transport problem analysis."[11] People, whose outlook and orientation is not confined within such a specific framework could possibly come up with unconventional or even novel ideas. But what is more important that their ideas are directly responsive to problems facing them. Development efforts from the people therefore could be valuable in qualitative terms as well.

In terms of the dimension of development, urban development is not only a matter of physical improvement and innovation. It is to be viewed within a holistic human development perspective. The scope of development signifies that an integrated approach is required to respond to different social needs which include access to income, employment opportunities, education, health, and a civil politico-cultural environment. Seen from this angle, the areas of works could be inexhaustible. Works, from within and without the mandates of the concerned authorities, will always be there to be accomplished, or better accomplished.

Furthermore, as civility is highly desirable in urban development, unified efforts derived from the authority's understanding and the people's outlook have become necessary. In place of coercive civility, civility based on law backed by state power, could result in consensual civility, guided by reason, moral sense, and social discipline. "Laws play but a minor part in people's behaviours, it would be far better to emphasize awareness building," succinctly expressed and wholeheartedly agreed by a group of stakeholders.

VI. PROPOSED ACTIONS

It is a widely held view that the independence of people's organizations is dependent on a non-interference policy of the authority. However, it does not follow that the former should be left entirely to their own resources, which are generally meagre. A genuine form of support for independence is also possible, if it is to be conducive and facilitating to socially purposeful people's activities.

The support can be either in cash or in kind as long as both are kept in line with the well-publicized slogan "helping people to help themselves" in general. Community Development Funds with an initial injection of cash from the central authorities could be established. These funds could be replenished from charges for services provided by revenue earning projects or local fund raising activities for "social projects". Such cash injections could help start projects getting off the ground.

Regarding help in kind, it could be either in the form of expertise (for example, providing expert services in the areas of public health measures, 'on-site' waste water treatment, sports training, etc.), or tangible assistances (e.g., meeting facilities, project loans, do-it-yourself materials). Such assistance can be made available on request. "Government agencies should make known to the people that they are ready to help... They could also partially help with the budget...loans to start small-scale commercial undertakings, for example. BMA may follow the example of the Department of Social Welfare, giving loans to the people in need. "They could give advice on the market situation, sources of investment, employment opportunities, etc."

A. A set of actions

(1)   Making a classification of activities that qualify for support. For project selection, multiple criteria should be adopted, so that they can be sufficiently comprehensive to accommodate a wide range of activities and also can consider the potentials of the people. The criteria can take into account of (a) issues and interests, e.g., environment, community empowerment, (b) social groups, e.g. youth, senior people, gender, (c) sector, e.g., economic, religious, (d) location, etc. Obviously different criteria serve different purposes. Different activities may be suitable for different age groups. The youth can devote themselves to the promotion of the use of bicycles and organization of walk rallies or public rallies against drug abuse, whereas the senior citizen groups can work in the areas of transfer of knowledge, and studies of the past. The issue-oriented activities can be at the micro and macro levels. Ecologism, environmentalism, for example, are advocated at the macro level, and implemented at the micro level.

(2)   Making announcements to the public to submit proposals for assistance. Announcements could be made at all three levels, namely, the city, the district and the sub-district. Particularly at the sub-district level, the authority can provide the necessary support in submitting proposals in two ways. The usual setting of office environment is the first system where the concerned officials can help the people to submit proposals at their offices. The second system is less conventional, and requires the officials to go out meeting people in

the communities, and serving those who require explanations and help in writing proposals. Both the in-house and out-reach receptions, though run with different degrees of activeness by the authority, adhere to the same principle of accommodating people's wishes.

(3)   Making budget allocation and public facilities available and making rules/regulations more friendly for people-run projects. Simultaneously, preventive measures against irregularities are necessary. Collective accountability by the working members of a given project has proved to be among the best practices. Assistance, financial or otherwise, may be given not to one or more individual(s), but to the group with the acknowledgement of all people concerned.

(4)   Making decisions by means of participatory approaches. To avoid favouritism, bureaucratic biases and other unfair practices, the mandate to approve project proposals should be given to neutral committees, elected from an agreed list of people respected within the community. On the basis of available resources, priorities should be given to proposals conforming to the rationales. The criteria for prioritisation should, therefore, not necessarily be restricted to economic viability and productivity, they need to include social justice, equality, sustainability and the principle of participation as well.

(5)   Making projects with lessons from well known good practices. To dispel scepticism and cynicism, it is useful to educate the public, the bureaucracy and other communities by exemplary cases. There have already been some highly recognized projects whose ethical codes of conduct and management are beyond question. With a reasonable degree of publicity, other current and future projects could follow their examples, and thereby unfavourable attitudes towards people's projects could be won over.

(6)   Making forums for conflict resolution. As conflicts could be aggravated and get out of control, forums of different sizes are highly commendable. A small-scale forum is to function at the sub-district level. The sub-district forums could be federated for conflict management at the district level. The forum may not assume a full legal status, it may only be formed on the basis of an administrative regulation. Personal integrity would be an important criterion for membership of the forum. People of proven integrity recognized by communities should be appointed and given the mandate of conflict management. The core function is not to impose definite decisions on parties in conflict. It is rather to settle differences in an amicable manner. For more serious cases, it is to focus on the domain of arbitration. At the city level, presumably issues are more complicated, in-depth studies could be conducted and impartial public hearings may be organized before important decisions are made.

CONCLUSIONS

People's initiatives in development can be valuable in both quantitative and qualitative terms. They could possibly come up with unconventional or even innovative ideas. What is more important that the people are more aware about their problems and their ideas are directly responsive to those problems. As such, institutional support needs to be provided by authorities to harness the potentials of the people and to facilitate people's ideas come to fruition.

SUGGESTED READINGS

Although the role of people have been advocated and recognized in the process of democratic development, it remains an important question as to how best they are to be actualised. Ready-made answers are too general for complex circumstances. But leaving people to their own devices is tantamount to negligence. Based on gainful experiences and past lessons, a wide variety of publications are available on strategies for participation. Selected below are only a few examples, which are not meant as models to be followed, let alone replicated, but as initial resources for modification, if not transformation. Full references are provided in the bibliography at the end of this report.

(1)   *Empowering People: A Guide to Participation* redresses the problems of application of people's participation by 'thinking through' the process. Important among the topics are the discussions on methods of promoting participation, monitoring and evaluation of participation, and institutional support for participation. The bibliography at the end is useful for academic as much as practical purposes.

(2)   *The World Bank Participation Sourcebook* is perhaps one among the best of its kind. Instead of 'preaching' or 'teaching' to readers about matters important in participatory processes, it is a collection of cases concretely experienced by participation practitioners. These stories of both 'successes and frustrations' are written as if field notes directly giving local and situation flavours. Generally its style of writing, intentionally or not, induces readers to reflect on their own works. Ideas to come from the book are therefore not directly from the pages, but through dialogues between the writers and the readers.

(3)   *Report and proceedings of the workshop on the use of urban forums as consultative mechanisms for urban planning and policy making* is a brief record of organized activities by people's functional groups, called in this context "citizen forums", in six cities, including Bangkok. It gives ideas and areas of activities together with some background information from which future actions can take benefits. More importantly, it provides a comparative perspective and a synthesis of diverse experiences. It is useful as a convenient start.

(4)   *Public Participation: Approaches in Urban Development Planning and Management* is a training material as well as a conceptual and practical framework for policy implementation. Extremely readable and specifically focused, this working paper is written with the conviction of decentralization and participation, and with the aim of practical application. It traces the development in the past and the present situation, and leads to prospective actions. Its main portion is devoted to what to do and how to proceed step by step including key elements, issues and guidelines to be borne in mind while pursuing the objectives of each step. It is a manual of high practical value.

STAKEHOLDERS' REFERENCES (FEW)

060116   Facilitate public participation in the conservation and development.

070507   Build motivation and imagination to love and care for surrounding areas and their resources, which should be taken most advantages of. Develop participation in urban planning,

E100113   Need to give incentives to people to maintain the charm of the locations and extend it to the adjacent areas. People should be encouraged to take more pride in their areas...If the original residents move out of the Area, Rattanakosin Area will loose its soul. People who live in the Area should be more involved in protecting its soul.

080105   We can offer ideas to the administrators.

090104   Promote the use of public opinions.

021601   Private sectors may give conveniences to the public.

140106   Provide opportunities for people who have capacities and understand problems to solve the problems. May be the private sector can solve problems faster and more efficiently than the government sectors.

Endnotes

[1] Nigel Harris (ed.), *Cities in the 1990s: The challenge for developing countries*, Overseas Development Administration, Development Planning Unit, University College London, 1992.

[2] To list only some of the well-known publications:

Faculty of Architecture, Silpakorn University, 1999. *The Project on Specific Location Planning in Historical Areas Project: Tha Prachan Community*, Report submitted to City Planning Division, Bangkok Metropolitan Administration (BMA), (in Thai).

Faculty of Architecture, King Mongkut Institute of Technology at Ladkrabang (KMITL),1999. *The Project on Specific Location Planning in Historical Areas Project: Tha Teian-Paklong Thalad*, Report submitted to City Planning Division, BMA, (in Thai).

Khankaew Yongprayoon, 1995. *The Project on the Development of Outer Rattanakosin Island with Specific Reference to the Northern Part of Rachadamnoen Klang Avenue,* Department of Design and Urban Community Planning, Graduate School, Silpakorn University, (in Thai).

Office of the Committee for Conservation and Development of Krung Rattanakosin and Old Towns, 1996. *Rattanakosin Project*, Office of Environmental Policy and Planning, Ministry of Science, Technology and Environment, (in Thai).

Office of the Committee for Conservation and Development of Krung Rattanakosin and Old Towns, 1996. *The Master Plan for Conservation and Development of Krung*

Rattanakosin, Office of Environmental Policy and Planning, Ministry of Science, Technology and Environment, (in Thai with English Translation).

Syncharon Group Co., Ltd., 1994. *Project on Master Plan and Action Plan Formulation on Conservation and Development of Thonburi Area Opposite to Krung Rattanakosin,* Report submitted to Office of Environmental Policy and Planning, Ministry of Science, Technology and Environment, (in Thai).

Syncharon Group Co., Ltd., 1994. *Master Plan on Conservation and Development of Rattanakosin Area*, Report submitted to Office of Environmental Policy and Planning, Ministry of Science, Technology and Environment, (in Thai).

Syncharon Group Co., Ltd., 1999. *Master Plan on Development of Public Utility System and Public Use in Rattanakosin Area*, Report submitted to Office of Environmental Policy and Planning, Ministry of Science, Technology and Environment, (in Thai).

[3] To name only some of the studies and reports related to the issues of transport carried out in the last decade.

Bangkok Mass Transit Authority (BMTA), 1998. *Annual Report 1998 Bangkok Mass Transit Authority*, Bangkok, Thailand.

Bangkok Metropolitan Administration (BMA), 1992. *The Bangkok General* Plan, Bangkok, Thailand.

Bangkok Metropolitan Administration (BMA), 1995. *A Vision for Bangkok: The Bangkok Plan, The Study of Bangkok Comprehensive Structure Plan and Conceptual Plan for Subcenters of Bangkok Metropolis*, A collaborative planning project of the Department of Planning, the MIT Consulting Team and the EC/BMA Project Team, Bangkok, Thailand.

Dorsch Consult, Louis Berger International, Epsilon, Tesco, MVA Asia, and Sofretu, 1998. *The Transport Planning and Policy Project*, Final Report Submitted to Office of the Commission for the Management of Land Traffic (OCMLT), Bangkok, Thailand.

Halcrow Fox and Associates, in Association with Pak Poy and Kneebone Pty Ltd. and Asian Engineering Consultants Corp. Lt., 1990. *Seventh Plan of Urban and Regional Transport* (SPURT), Final Report Submitted to the Office of National Economic and Social Development Board (NESDB), Bangkok, Thailand.

Japan International Cooperation Agency (JICA), 1997. *Technical Assistance for Urban Traffic and Transportation Planning*, Final Report Prepared for OCMLT, Bangkok, Thailand.

Japan International Cooperation Agency (JICA), 1997. *Urban Traffic Plan in Bangkok Metropolitan Region*, Final Report, Prepared for OCMLT, Bangkok, Thailand.

Leman Group, 1994. *Metropolitan Regional Structure Planning Study,* Report Submitted to NESDB of Thailand, Toronto, Canada.

Wilbur Smith Associates Inc. et al, 1994. *Mass Rapid Transit Systems Master Plan,* Final Report Submitted to OCMLT, Bangkok, Thailand.

World Bank, 1999. *Bangkok Urban Transport Sector Review,* Draft Report.

[4]   Gary Craig et Marjorie Mayo (eds.),1995. *Community Empowerment,* Zed Books, London.

[5]   The Community Development Department of the Ministry of Interior makes extensive use of the A-I-C
(Appreciation – Influence- Control) participatory approach.

[6]   United Nations Development Programme (UNDP), 1997. *Reonceptualising Governance,* New York, p. 10.

[7]   (*Bangkok Post*, September 3, 2000).

[8]   A government project loan for community development in 1999.

[9]   David Harvey, 1989. *The Urban Experience*, Johns Hopkins University press, Baltimore, p. 228.

[10] Nigel Harris, op. cit., p. 179.

[11] Harry T. Dimitriou, 1995. *A Developmental Approach to Urban Transport Planning,* Avebury, Sydney, p. 55.

PART II

Technical Action Plans

INTRODUCTION

The second part of this report deals with specific actions to be undertaken to address some of the major issues and problems mainly related to traffic and transportation in Rattanakosin Area. This part contains twelve integrated action plans designed to deal with the major issues identified by the stakeholders which include improvement of public transportation, pedestrian freedom, traffic restraint, poor habits of road use, parking, etc. The action plans have been formulated to address the identified issues in a comprehensive and integrated manner. Because of their "symbiotic" relationship, the plans are mutually inclusive and as such effectiveness of the individual plans depends much on the totality of their implementation simultaneously. They should be considered together and not one without the others. The twelve integrated action plans are as follow:

- Road Classification
- Pedestrian-friendly Roads and Streets
- Improvement of Bus Service
- Integration of Public Transport
- Traffic Restraint and Demand Management
- Comprehensive Parking Policy
- School Travel Plans
- Traffic Calming in Rattankosin
- Community Traffic Warden Programme
- Correction of Poor Road Using Habits
- Commuting from the Thonburi side of the Chao Phrya River
- People's Collective and Shared Responsibility for the Development of Rattanakosin

It is important to mention here that these twelve action plans are based on the process pursued within the Rattanakosin Pilot Project, i.e., stakeholders' views, which were originally collected through interviews and that were expressed in different workshops at later dates, and problem and cause analysis based on those views. Supplementary information from secondary sources was gathered in support of stakeholders' views and to verify consistency with other plans and actions that are being implemented or are under consideration by different authorities.

Each of the action plans has fourteen sections describing different aspects of the plan. Section I gives the title of the plan. A brief description of the current situation based on stakeholders' narration and supplementary information from secondary sources is presented in Section II. Major issues and problems, which emerged from the problem and cause analysis and reformulation of stakeholders' views, are mentioned in Section III. Section IV provides the proposed actions to deal with the problems and issues as suggested by the stakeholders. Relationships to previous plans are mentioned in Section V. Expected impact of the actions, as visualised by the stakeholders, are presented in Section VI. The identified beneficiary groups from the actions are mentioned in Section VII. The direct activities to be undertaken are outlined in Section VIII. These activities are related to the actions identified by the stakeholders and as presented in Section IV. Section IX identifies the authorities/ groups/alliances to implement the plan. External factors and constraints for implementation are mentioned in Section X. Section XI provides monitoring indicators and briefly mentions how the success of the plan may be evaluated. Relationships to other action plans are mentioned in Section XII. Further studies required are mentioned in Section XIII. Finally, Section XIV provides a few examples of stakeholders' references concerning the issues and their suggested actions.

The following sections of the report describe each of those twelve action plans in turn.

ROAD CLASSIFICATION

Pedestrian Street

Soi/Access Road

Local Road

Secondary Road

Primary Road

ACTION PLAN 01

I. TITLE OF THE ACTION PLAN

Road Classification

II. BACKGROUND

The major functions performed by urban roads can be broadly categorized as access, circulation of local and through traffic, and environmental improvement. A particular road may not need to perform all these functions. However, for the purposes of planning and design, the functions that a road should cater for need to be identified and relevant priorities should be assigned to it. Otherwise, conflicts arise when a road cannot accommodate the competing demands. The typical traffic problems in Rattanakosin area are often caused by a whole range of conflicting road uses and the cyclical impacts which they have on one another.

Pedestrian activity is very intensive in many parts of Rattanakosin, which requires a pedestrian-friendly environment free from hazards of fast moving traffic. On the other hand, certain roads in the area also need to function as traffic corridors to allow safe and fast passage of a large volume of through traffic passing through the area. Because of these conflicting demands of road uses and limited capacity of the road network in Rattanakosin, it is important to determine which of the various demands should be given priority, considering the most appropriate role of a road in question and its relationship with other roads. As has been observed by some stakeholders, "BMA should consider which road should have what kind of traffic".

Priorities for certain kinds of traffic or types of use can be given in a variety of ways ranging from physical design of road elements to regulatory measures. When roads are categorized according to their priority functions, a hierarchy of road systems follows. It may be mentioned here that physical size of a road does not define its position in the hierarchy. In a hierarchical system, important distributors feed down through distributors of a lesser category to the minor roads which give access to buildings. The system may be linked to the trunk, limbs, branches, and finally the twigs of a tree. The major benefits of establishing a road hierarchy are as follows:

- The capacity of major traffic routes can be increased.

- Road safety can be improved.

- Activities incompatible with traffic flow can be restricted on designated routes.

- The overall impact of traffic can be reduced by channelizing major flows into fewer routes.

- Environmental, access and other functions of lower category roads can be improved.

- Implementation of traffic management measures can be easier.

Considering the benefits of road classification, a classification scheme with five types of roads, their physical features and functions is proposed as presented in Table 1.

III. MAJOR ISSUES AND PROBLEMS

At present the roads and streets in the area are not classified to prioritise certain functions. As a result most of the roads cater for all the competing functions in an uncontrolled way, which has lead to:

1)   Conflicts in road uses.
2)   Congestion on major traffic routes and slow passage of through traffic.
3)   Traffic hazards in pedestrian activity areas.
4)   Poor environmental and access conditions.

IV. PROPOSED ACTIONS

1)   Classification of all roads and streets in Rattanakosin area according to their functions and following a classification scheme as proposed in Table 1.
2)   Implementation of physical, environmental and traffic management measures appropriate for each category of roads.

V. RELATIONSHIP TO PREVIOUS PLANS

The JICA study of 1997 discussed the current types of roads and a classification system in Bangkok but did not consider any specific proposal for road classification.

VI. EXPECTED IMPACT AND RESULTS

1)   Reduced traffic congestion and improvement of the overall environmental condition.
2)   Increased attractiveness of the area to visitors.
3)   Better pedestrian friendly environment, supportive to community activities.
4)   Improved access to cultural and heritage sites, and shopping districts.
         Improved road safety.

VII. BENEFICIARY GROUPS

This plan is expected to benefit all residents in general, people who work and do business in the area, visitors, and other road users who pass through the area.

Table 1. Proposed hierarchical classification of roads based on their functions

Road			Function						Allowable speed
Type	Physical features	Major purpose	Pedestrian	Parking	Vehicular access to abutting properties	Circulation of local traffic	NMV	Trough traffic	
Pedestrian Street	Can be of any width with full range of street furniture, closed to vehicular traffic during activity hours or permanently or open only to public transport	Walking Meeting Vending/ Trading	Complete freedom for pedestrians	Not allowed except for service vehicles (short duration)	Not allowed	Not allowed	Bicycles may be allowed	Not allowed	Does not apply (essentially free of motorized vehicular traffic)
Soi/Access Road	5-7 m. wide with traffic calming measures; may have footpath	Walking NMVs Vehicular access	Freedom with no control on crossing; Footpath at least on one side preferable	Generally allowed subject to safety requirements and width of road	Predominant function	Limited to facilitate movement within the neighbourhood and to local centre	Allowed; can form a part of local NMV network	Not allowed	20 Kph
Local Road	8-10 m. wide with footpath and traffic calming measures	Channelisation of vehicular traffic between access road and secondary roads; small vehicle public transport services	Freedom with some control on crossings; Footpath on both sides preferable	Allowed	Allowed	Predominant function	Allowed, can form a part of local NMV network	Not allowed	30 Kph
Secondary Road	4-6 lanes with footpaths; single or dual carriage-way; controlled pedestrian crossings with refuge areas	Medium-distance traffic, all through traffic, bus services	Controlled with positive measures for their safety: where possible vertical segregation preferred	May be allowed at off-peak hours; and on weekends depending on traffic flow	Allowed only to major centres having vehicular flow equivalent to a local road	Some - only few localities may be served	May be allowed, preferably with physical segregation	Predominantly serve medium distance traffic	40-50 Kph
Primary Road	6 or more lanes; dual carriageway; segregated pedestrian crossings	Fast moving long-distance traffic preferably with no/limited frontage access	Fully controlled, and vertically segregated from vehicular traffic	Not allowed	Generally not allowed except to city-level activity centres	Very little, (should have limited crossings to discourage local traffic)	May be allowed in selected sections with full physical segregation	Predominant function	>70 Kph depending on road geometry and traffic condition

Note: Number of lanes of secondary and primary roads depends primarily on volume of traffic and allowable speed.

VIII. ACTIVITIES TO BE UNDERTAKEN

The activities to be undertaken to implement this Action Plan are as follows:

1) Undertake a comprehensive traffic study in the area to determine volume and pattern of flow.
2) Identify areas with intensive pedestrian activities.
3) Identify pedestrian-only roads.
4) Designate primary roads to cater for through traffic.
5) Establish middle-order secondary and local roads.
6) Create pedestrian and NMV flow networks.
7) Secure support from the community and others concerned to implement pedestrian-only streets, and to remove activities incompatible with the primary function of a particular road.
8) Relocate the removed activities to other appropriate roads/places.
9) Apply sensitive surface treatment and provide street furniture (street lights, pedestrian protection fences, telephone booths, etc.) appropriate to indicate priority functions of different roads.
10) Install appropriate traffic management devices/measures.

Other supporting/complementary activities:

1) Restructuring of public transport routes.
2) Control of goods vehicles in pedestrianized areas.

IX. RESPONSIBLE AUTHORITY/GROUPS/ALLIANCES

Responsible authority/groups:

Bangkok Metropolitan Authority (BMA)
Bangkok Mass Transit Authority (BMTA)
Police Department
Vendors
Local communities

Alliances:

Department of Town and City Planning
Office of the Commission for the Management of Land Traffic (OCMLT)

X. EXTERNAL FACTORS, CONSTRAINTS, AND PREREQUISITES

1) Relocation of incompatible road uses.
2) Direct community support and active participation to implement actions including closure/limiting of vehicular access to particular roads and other pedestrianization measures that restrict direct vehicular access to individual properties.

XI. MONITORING AND EVALUATION

Monitoring indicators:

Presence of through traffic on lower order roads
Travel speed on major traffic routes
Perception of traffic hazards
Incidence of traffic accidents

Success evaluation:

An ex-post evaluation can be made by conducting a traffic survey to determine if 1) through traffic exists in large number on lower category roads, 2) volume of traffic decreased on lower category roads, and 3) average speed on major traffic routes has increased. Significant positive changes would indicate success of the plan.

XII. RELATIONSHIP TO OTHER PLANS

This plan has strong relationship to various actions under Action Plans 02, 05, 06, 08, and 11. The overall relationship is shown in Table 2.

XIII. REQUIRED FURTHER STUDIES

Detailed land use survey of the area
Inventory of road network
Volume and pattern (existing and desired) of traffic flow
Study on pedestrian flow

XIV. STAKEHOLDERS' REFERENCES (FEW EXAMPLES)

080105 BMA should consider which road should have what kind of traffic.
050102 Physical improvement is needed (improve road to good condition to ease flow of traffic).
040204 Build roads that do not come into the island or build elevated roads to reduce traffic problem.
040206 The cooperation must depend on one's consideration to avoid coming into the area especially people outside the area.
020101 Increase alternative ways for people to go to work without passing this area.
060202 Every road in Bangkok should be in order.
021303 Traffic system in Rattanakosin Island should be re-planned.
040102 Improve road surface and condition as much as possible to reduce traffic problem in the long run.
040105 Rearrange traffic system to avoid crossroads.
060116 Traffic system arrangement should be appropriate for each area, Traffic system arrangement and all facilities should be in accordance with land use.
150104 Promote better flow of traffic.
100113 If you want to protect the area then you must siphon off the through traffic.

Table 2. Relationship matrix between the plans (showing only strong and considerable relationship)

		Action Plan											
		01	02	03	04	05	06	07	08	09	10	11	12
Action Plan	01	-	++	+		++	++		++			++	+
	02	++	-	+			++	++	++	++	+		+
	03	+		-	++	++	+	+		+	+	++	+
	04			++	-	++	++	+				++	
	05	++		++	++	-	++	++				++	++
	06	++	++	+	+	++	-	+	+	++	++	++	
	07		++	+	+	++	+	-	++	++		+	++
	08	++	++				+	++	-		+		+
	09		++				++	++		-	++		++
	10		+	+			++		+	++	-		++
	11	++		++	++	++	++	+				-	+
	12	+	+	+		++		++	+	++	++	+	-

Notes: 01 = Road classification; 02 = Pedestrian street; 03 = Bus services; 04 = Integration of public transport; 05 = Transport demand management; 06 = Parking policy; 07 = School travel plan; 08 = Traffic calming; 09 = Community traffic warden; 10 = Road using habit; 11 = Commuting from the Thonburi side of the Chao Phrya River; 12 = Collective and Shared Responsibility

+ = Considerable relationship
++ = Strong relationship

PEDESTRAIN-FRIENDLY ROADS AND STREETS

ACTION PLAN 02

I. TITLE OF THE ACTION PLAN

Pedestrian-friendly Roads and Streets in Rattanakosin Area

II. BACKGROUND AND CURRENT SITUATION

Walking totals about 16per cent of all trips in Bangkok. The share of walking is, however, much lower compared with 27per cent in Tokyo, 25per cent in Singapore, and other cities in the region (JICA, 1997; Barter 1999). Apart from inclement weather conditions, there are many reasons for low preference to walking in Bangkok. Pedestrian spaces along the major streets are usually occupied for all types of vending, and various other activities and purposes, leaving inadequate and unpleasant spaces for pedestrians. It is also inconvenient to walk along many streets in Rattanakosin, and in general in Bangkok, for various other reasons such as poor surface condition of footpaths, inadequate pedestrian safety measures, obstructing stationary objects, heavy exhaust fumes and noise of roaring vehicles around. In an unpleasant environment, walking is largely discouraging, particularly for children, older people, people with disabilities, and parents with children, which motivates them to choosing a motorized mode even for short-distance trips. This in turn contributes to further worsening of traffic and environmental conditions of the area.

III. MAJOR ISSUES AND PROBLEMS

1) Unpleasant conditions and difficulties in walking along footpaths.
2) Lack of pedestrian freedom in the areas of intensive pedestrian activities.
3) Pedestrian safety.
4) Use of motorized modes for short-distance trips.
5) Pollution and inconvenience due to vendors and other incompatible uses of pedestrian areas.

IV. PROPOSED ACTIONS

1) Conversion of certain streets in Rattanakosin Area as "pedestrian-only" streets and some other streets with limited access to public transport modes only. Subject to further study of local circulation pattern, examples of streets for possible consideration are Pra Athit Road, Kao Sarn Road, and roads in Pahurat area.
2) Improvement of access to cultural heritage sites through interconnected pedestrian ways and where possible pedestrianization of the whole area in the vicinity of such sites.
3) Relocation of vendors from pedestrian areas in alternative sites close to the existing locations.
4) Action for pollution control and garbage collection in pedestrian areas.

5)   Greening along pedestrian areas and creation of spots with pedestrian interests by landscaping of unused pocket spaces (a good example to follow is the new *Phra Sumeru* Fortress Park by the river).

6)   Provision of well-designed pavements with ramps for the use of wheel chairs, prams, etc. and also provision of devices to assist people with sight or hearing impairments.

7)   Ensuring pedestrian safety through controlled crossings at zebra and signalized crossings, providing pedestrian refuges and implementing traffic calming measures (Action Plan 08) on the local streets.

8)   Ensuring personal safety along streets during fixing of utility lines such as electric cables, water lines, telephone wires, etc. from open/uncovered manholes, and replacement of damaged/missing manhole covers.

9)   Provision of covered walkways and planting of trees to protect pedestrians from direct sunlight and rain, and providing street furniture such as benches, telephone booths, special lighting, shelters, etc. along the footpaths and walkways to make walking attractive.

10)   Promotion of public awareness about walking and use of pedestrian areas through:

    a.   Public campaigns organized by BMA, NGOs, local schools and CBOs.
    b.   Use of the media.

11)   Organization of training programs:

    a.   Conducting traffic safety training workshops in schools and in the community.
    b.   Training for correcting poor road using habits (Action Plan 10).

V. RELATIONSHIP TO PREVIOUS PLANS

Some of the actions such as motorized mode free streets and improvement of access to cultural heritage sites through creation of pedestrian areas have been proposed in the plan made by the Rattanakosin Committee. BMA has also proposed special action for pollution control along pedestrian areas and greening along walkways. All these proposals are yet to be implemented. The proposed Action Pan incorporates these proposals and considers a few more actions to make the whole area pedestrian-friendly in a comprehensive way as well as to integrate actions for other purposes.

VI. EXPECTED IMPACT AND RESULTS

1)   Increased attractiveness of the area to the visitors.
2)   Improved access to cultural heritage sites and other sites with intensive pedestrian activities.
3)   Increased share of walking for short trips and using a combination of walking and public transport for long trips.
4)   Reduced traffic congestion and improvement of overall environment.
5)   Improved pedestrian freedom, and safety along streets.
6)   Increased social interaction in the communities.

VII. BENEFICIARY GROUPS

The action plan is aimed at short-distance trip makers among residents, shoppers, visitors, school children and people who work in the area. The plan would be appealing to visitors, large numbers of children and young adults, a significant portion of residents who are non-drivers and people who have an interest in improving their physical fitness. It is expected that people in the area will shift to walking from motorized modes for short-distance trips to work, shopping, school, or to get access to public transport modes. This action plan would not make any significant reduction of total vehicle mileage, but will help to revitalize the area by increasing its internal accessibility, attractiveness and liveability.

VIII. ACTIVITIES TO BE UNDERTAKEN

Direct Activities:

1) Investigate and determine predominant functions of the roads in the area following the classification criteria proposed under Action Plan 1 and plan them accordingly as vehicular or pedestrian priority roads.
2) Improve the surface condition, and ensure regular maintenance and cleaning of footpaths/walkways.
3) Undertake landscaping of footpaths/walkways and pocket spaces by the roads.
4) Consider relocation of vendors from narrow and busy footpaths/walkways and if possible, provide alternative sites for them by the roads.
5) Campaign and make publicity to create public attention and encourage community participation.
6) Prepare pedestrian route maps to important sites and places of interest.
7) Start a pilot project immediately with participation of local community and other stakeholders in planning and implementation of the project.

Supporting/complementary activities:

1) Promote walking to school by providing school travel plans and safe routes initiatives.
2) Integrate activities with access improvement to public transport.
3) Restrict motorbikes in the pedestrian areas.
4) Clearly state, publicize and strictly enforce delivery time for merchandise and goods to shops and properties on pedestrian-only streets.
5) Adopt pollution control measures.

Successful examples/models:

In recent years, pedestrianization schemes of city/town centres have attracted wide attention. Pedestrian zones have become a familiar feature in the central and residential areas of many world cities (for example, the "woonerven" system in Dutch cities). Apart from improvement of pedestrian facilities along the roads, a number of cities in many countries have implemented successfully the concept of a pedestrian-friendly environment on an area basis to facilitate pedestrian activities. One study found that residents in a pedestrian friendly community walked, bicycled, or rode transit more than residents of a comparable automobile oriented community (Cervero and Radisch, 1995)

The concept of pedestrianization is not totally new to Bangkok. Creating a pedestrian friendly environment has been experimented with in Rattanakosin area, too. Occasionally roads such as Pra Athit Road, Phra Sumen Road, Kao Sarn Road have been declared as walking streets to organize special events like fairs or cultural events. What has been proposed here subscribes to the same idea but in a more comprehensive way, and on a wider scale and permanent basis.

IX. RESPONSIBLE AUTHORITY/GROUPS/ALLIANCES:

Responsible Groups/Authority:

Bangkok Metropolitan Administration (BMA)
Bangkok Metropolitan Transport Authority (BMTA)
Local communities
Roadside vendors
Police Department
Schools and education authorities

Alliances:

Department of Town and City Planning
Office of the Commission for the Management of Land Traffic (OCMLT)

X. EXTERNAL FACTORS / CONSTRAINTS / PREREQUISITES

1)   Convincing street vendors and relocating them to other sites.
2)   Active participation and support of the communities is needed to plan and implement pedestrian walkways and converting an existing street to a pedestrian-only street.

XI. MONITORING AND EVALUATION

Monitoring indicators:

Share of walking trips
Number of pedestrians using a facility
Number of people walking to work, school, shopping, etc.
Number of accidents involving pedestrians
Level of service of pedestrian facilities (the standards set in the Highway Capacity Manual (Transportation Research Board, 1994) may be followed)

Success evaluation:

Evaluation of success can be done through quantitative and qualitative changes in the values of the indicators and from attitude surveys of residents, people who work in the area and visitors. Indicator values have to be gathered from traffic surveys.

XII. RELATIONSHIP TO OTHER PLANS

This plan has strong relationship to various actions under Action Plans 01, 06, 07, 08, and 09. The overall relationship is shown in Table 2.

XIII. REQUIRED FURTHER STUDIES AND INVESTIGATIONS

Vehicular and pedestrian traffic circulation pattern in the area
Possible impact of closing a street to vehicular traffic
Investigation of sites with pedestrian interests
Pedestrian preferences of facilities
Pedestrian flows in critical areas
Relocation of vendors

XIV. STAKEHOLDERS' REFERENCES (SOME EXAMPLES)

040303	Footpaths should be improved to be more beautiful and convenient.
040303	Improve pavement to promote walking instead of using cars and there should be activities held in communities to urge for public participation.
050102	Make this area a "walking area". No cars will be allowed except buses. Move the central market out. This will help solve the traffic and environmental problems.
070310	Houses and buildings should not be built near the street in order to have more space for people to walk and to grow trees. Building owners should devote some space to extend the walkways.
070509	Establish car free zones to allow easy flow of people and have many kinds of activities together.
100101	Prepare a useful and clear city plan for this area. Promote entering this area by foot and improve pavement to be more beautiful and provide a lot of tourist facilities such as toilets and souvenir shops.
120103	Construct more walkways.
020503	Go by foot if it's not too far.
021001	Keep pavement always clean.
060208	Walking streets have the atmosphere of the old city with a walkway along the river, coffee shop, shops and places for relaxing which are peaceful like Singapore, Santa Monica.
E100109	It would be nice if arrangements could be made to allow tourists and pedestrians to enjoy walking in this area, and create bicycle routes and parks. I know this would not be feasible for the whole Bangkok. But for Rattanakosin, considering its tourist attractions, it is worth to try.
022205	Environmental condition should be improved e.g. planting more trees that will give more shade to the city and make the air cleaner.
150109	Trees should be planted along the roads especially along Rajadamnern Avenue.
070510	Increase public parks along side of the Chao Phraya River. Increase green areas. Conserve old houses and buildings

040303	There should be basic infrastructure for pedestrians e.g. phone booths, trash bins, and streetlights should be continuous and maintained.
022402	There should be public drink fountains and toilets in crowded areas.
020601	Provide enough garbage bins in the right spots for tourists' convenience.

REFERENCES/OTHER STUDIES

Barter, Paul, 1999. *An International Comparative Perspective on Urban Transport and Urban Form in Pacific Asia: The Challenge of Rapid Motorisation in Dense Cities*, PhD Thesis, MURDOCH University, Australia.

Cervero, Robert and Carolyn Radisch, 1995. *Travel Choices in Pedestrian Verses Automobile Oriented Neighborhoods*, UC Transport Centre, UCTC 281 (socrates.berkeley.edu/~uctc).

Department of the Environment, Transport and the Regions, 2000. *Encouraging Walking: Advice to local authorities*, United Kingdom. *(www.local_transport.gov.uk/)*

Japan International Cooperation Agency, 1997. *Final Report on Technical Assistance for Urban Traffic and Transport Planning,* prepared for The Office of the Commission for the Management of Land Traffic, Bangkok, Thailand.

Transportation Research Board, 1994. *Highway Capacity Manual*, Special Report 209, Washington, D.C.

Victoria Transport Policy Institute, 2000. *Pedestrian and Bicycle Planning: A Guide to Best Practices*, Canada.

IMPROVEMENT OF BUS SERVICE

ACTION PLAN 03

I. TITLE OF THE ACTION PLAN

Improvement of Bus Service in Rattanakosin.

II. BACKGROUND AND CURRENT SITUATION

Buses are considered as the main workhorse of urban transport in Bangkok. They carried 41per cent of total passengers (about 5.2 million bus passengers a day) in 1995 compared with 23per cent by car, 14per cent by motorcycle, 5per cent by taxi, and about 15per cent by walking and other modes. The combined share of trips by railway and ferry was only about 2per cent (JICA, 1997). The bus transport would continue to remain as the main mode of transport despite the facts that its level of service is not very satisfactory, and an elevated rail mass transit system was introduced in 2000 and another underground rail transit system is under construction. As the rail transit systems will not be accessible to all public transport users and the combined capacity of the rail systems (existing and planned) would be far less than the total demand for public transport services, there would always be a need for good bus services.

Efforts have been made from time to time to improve the level of service of bus operation. Among other measures, bus lanes were introduced on major roads in the early 1980s. However, because of poor enforcement, effective operation of bus lanes is very rare. During times of heavy traffic congestion, buses are stranded and subject to long delays as they share the same right of way with other vehicles.

Measures have also been taken to improve riding comfort by introducing new buses. To minimize poor air quality problems, Bangkok Mass Transit Authority (BMTA) has been operating natural gas buses (NGV) on an experimental basis since 1992. By 1999, 82 natural gas buses were operating along three different routes originating from Rangsit, where the only refuelling station is located. Apart from lack of refuelling facilities, NGV buses are more expensive than similar diesel buses. These facts limit the provision of more NGV buses. BMTA has also rented 797 Euro II buses with higher emission control standards. Some of these buses have arrangements for wheel chair lifting to provide easy access for people with disabilities.

Lack of ancillary facilities such as public toilets at the major bus stops and at the end points of many bus routes is another problem in Rattanakosin. This is not directly related to bus transport, but causes inconvenience to road users and bus crew. It is seen in many places that bus crew use side walks or nearby *klongs* to relieve the call of nature resulting in water pollution, bad smell and danger to public health.

Enhancement of the quality of bus and other public transport services is not an end in itself. It is a prerequisite to look for any general improvement of the traffic and transportation situation in Rattanakosin or for that matter in the whole city. As mentioned by a stakeholder, "…If the city improves its mass transport system, people will use this kind of transport which can help decrease traffic congestion".

III. MAJOR ISSUES AND PROBLEMS

1) The levels of service in terms of journey and waiting time, on-board crowding, reliability, etc. are not satisfactory.
2) Ineffectiveness of bus lanes during peak hours.
3) Transfer tickets are not available and often transfer points to other routes are not direct and convenient.
4) Lack of integration with other public transport modes.
5) The proportion of buses with easy access facilities for people with disabilities is low.
6) Inadequate bus stop facilities such as sheltered waiting areas, toilets, etc.

IV. PROPOSED ACTIONS

1) Urgent restructuring and reorganization of the existing "destination oriented" bus routes, which originated basically as accidents of history, into "direction oriented" bus routes with integrated feeder and corridor services. This action is crucial to any significant improvement of bus services.
2) Introduction of new bus routes for movement within Rattanakosin providing frequent services preferably with smaller natural gas vehicles and with smooth transfer points to other corridor routes, BTS stations, and boat piers.
3) Establishment of more refueling stations for NGV buses with one in Rattanakosin.
4) Issuance of transfer tickets between bus routes and development of transfer points for easy transfer to other routes and modes with possible transfer locations at Hualumpong, Victory Monument, Sanam Luang, PATA Pinklao, Bangkok Noi Railway station, etc.
5) Implementation and enforcement of effective bus lanes on all major roads in Rattanakosin.
6) Introduction of more NGV buses, and rapid phasing out of the existing non-Euro standard bus fleet with Euro II or higher emission control standard buses
7) Provision of more buses with easy access facilities for people with disabilities.
8) Provision of ancillary facilities at the major bus stops.
9) Introduction of a real-time bus operational management system.

V. RELATIONSHIP TO PREVIOUS PLANS

It is understood that BMTA is currently studying the possibility of introducing transfer tickets between routes. Introduction of transfer tickets would be needed before any overall reorganization of bus routes can be effected with direction oriented major routes directly served by destination oriented local feeder routes at convenient transfer points. Proposals have also been made to consider a reorganization of bus routes to avoid duplication of services and extension of the area served directly. It is also understood that BMA is currently considering reorginzation of bus routes following the principle outlined in proposed action IV (1).

Bus lanes already exist in Bangkok. Proposals have been made for their extension in Rattanakosin and for enforcement to make them effective.

VI. EXPECTED IMPACT AND RESULTS

1) Improved level of bus service.
2) Reduced traffic congestion.
3) Increased accessibility of the area.
4) Decrease in air quality problems.
5) Improved access to public transport for people with disabilities.

VII. BENEFICIARY GROUPS

Major beneficiary groups of the plan include bus users of Bangkok, visitors and the people who live and work in Rattanakosin.

VIII. ACTIVITIES TO BE UNDERTAKEN

Direct Activities:

1) Conduct an O-D survey of bus passengers in Rattanakosin.
2) Totally restructure the existing bus routes to provide express corridor services served by local feeder routes, and integrated with BTS train and the Chao Phraya boat services (refer to Action Plan 04).
3) Introduce smaller vehicles with high emission control standards for bus operation on the reorganized local/feeder routes in Rattanakosin area.
4) Designate bus lanes in the area with clear signs, markings, etc.
5) Publicize widely the introduction of new bus lanes and enforce operation of existing and new bus lanes by employing local traffic wardens (Action Plan 09) and installing devices to deter intruders into bus lanes.
6) Examine if certain streets can be designated as bus-only streets.
7) Subject to city-wide bus route reorganization, examine if some of the routes can be redirected to enable faster bus operation through the area with direct participation of bus passengers and crew members.
8) Develop convenient transfer points between routes and interchange facilities with other modes of (public) transport.

Supporting/complementary activities:

1) Efforts to integrate public transport modes with participation of all operators.
2) Enforcement of traffic law.
3) Training for correction of poor road using habits of bus and car drivers.

Successful examples/models:

Hong Kong, Singapore, and Curitiba in Brazil provide good models of urban bus service operation.

IX. RESPONSIBLE AUTHORITY/GROUPS/ALLIANCES

Responsible Authority:

Bangkok Mass Transit Authority (BMTA)
Bangkok Metropolitan Administration (BMA)
Department of Land Transport
Police Department
Local communities

Alliances:

Commuters in Rattanakosin Area
Office of the Commission for the Management of Land Traffic (OCMLT)

X. EXTERNAL FACTORS/CONSTRAINTS/PREREQUISITES

Reorganization of bus routes and integration with other public transport modes are the two essential elements in improving bus services in the area and in Bangkok in general. However, these problems have to be handled at the city level. As most of the bus routes are not confined just within Rattanakosin, route reorganization has to be implemented at the city level. Similarly, many of the possible transfer points are located outside the area and integration with other modes would require direct participation of all public transport operators operating outside Rattanakosin.

XI. MONITORING INDICATORS AND EVALUATION

Monitoring indicators:

Increase in level of bus ridership
Increase in average bus speed and reliability
Waiting time, transfer time
Opinion of bus passengers on level of service
Number of Euro II or higher emission control standard buses

Evaluation:

Establish benchmarks and collect information on performance indicators on a regular basis to judge the success of the plan.

XII. RELATIONSHIP TO OTHER PLANS

This plan has strong relationship to various actions under Action Plans 04, 05, and 11.

XIII. REQUIRED FURTHER STUDIES AND INVESTIGATIONS

An O-D survey of bus passengers
Study on restructuring of bus routes
Study on improvement of bus operation
Information on bus routes, bus stops, transfer points
Study on issuance of transfer tickets
Study on cooperation between different service operators to provide an integrated public transport service
Operational analysis of bus lanes

XIV. STAKEHOLDERS' REFERENCES (SOME EXAMPLES)

050103   Improve public mass transport to have good quality and sufficient services and must not cause air pollution. If the city improves mass transport system, people will use this kind of transport which can help decrease traffic congestion.

060115   Develop public transport to be better (punctual and certain), people will stop using private cars but it must have complementary measures to prohibit private cars in the area. If the public transport is good, traffic will be good, too.

040203   Solve the traffic problem by promoting mass transit system.

080202   Improve mass transit system to be more modern and more comfortable.

080201   The issue of public transport should be considered seriously.

130106   Mass transport is insufficient.

040406, 0700503, 070508, 140102 Increase the number of buses and improve their services.

020401   Increase the number of buses. It is difficult for people to commute.

070312   Change old buses to EURO II buses.

090103   Increase public transport systems.

070509   Provide parking spaces for car users and let car users use public buses.

060207   Improve mass transit system in every aspect to be more effective.

070314   It would be great if there is a bus lane project so that buses can flow easily.

030401   Should develop traffic systems to make bus lane more important and vehicles should be regulated to use the correct lane.

100108   Drivers use the road improperly and always drive between two lanes while buses are not in the bus lane.

070314   Private cars run in bus lanes.

REFERENCES

Japan International Cooperation Agency, 1997. *Final Report on Technical Assistance for Urban Traffic and Transport Planning,* prepared for The Office of the Commission for the Management of Land Traffic, Bangkok, Thailand.

INTEGRATION OF PUBLIC TRANSPORT

ACTION PLAN 04

I. TITLE OF THE ACTION PLAN

Integration of Public Transport

II. BACKGROUND AND CURRENT SITUATION

Bangkok is served by a wide variety of public and private transport modes. The public transport modes include buses of various types, rail transit, boats and ferries, and a wide range of paratransit modes including taxis, samlors, silors, and hired motorcycles. However, organized facilities to allow a convenient interchange between different modes of public transport need to be improved and/or developed. Very often, there is no direct interface between two public transport modes or even between two bus routes. Consequently, passengers desiring transfer from one mode to another face difficulties in getting on to the next mode to continue their journeys.

The situation in Rattanakosin is no different from other locations in Bangkok. The area is served directly by a number of bus routes many of which originate in the area, boat services along Chao Phraya river, informal transport, and paratransit modes, and indirectly by the recently introduced BTS rail transit system. There is lack of integration of these modes. There is considerable scope of enhancing the utility of public transport systems and hence motivating people to using them if all these different systems can be integrated to facilitate unimpeded movement of passengers across the city. An integrated system would also help improve the accessibility of the area and its overall transportation condition.

While integrating the bus and boat transport, it is important to link this with riverfront development to conserve the environment and at the same time address wider community needs.

III. MAJOR ISSUES AND PROBLEMS

1) Lack of complementary services by different transit modes.
2) Poor condition of bus/boat interchanges and only few boat piers are directly connected to bus routes.
3) Integration of bus services with the rail transit systems (new, under construction and proposed).
4) Organization of informal modes of public transport to provide feeder services to transit modes (bus, boat, and rail systems).

IV. PROPOSED ACTIONS

1) Restructuring of bus routes to provide separate fast corridor services and frequent local/feeder services for integration with corridor bus services and other transit modes (refer to Action Plan 03).

2)   Local reorganization of bus routes to facilitate direct connection with all the boat piers in Rattanakosin which are served by express, ferry and long-tail boat services along Chao Phraya river.

3)   Introduction of new bus routes with environmentally friendly smaller vehicles for movement within Rattanakosin and providing frequent feeder services to the rail transit systems (present and future) and boat piers (also see Action Plan 03).

4)   Initiation of steps towards a common ticketing system for the feeder bus services and the rail transit system(s). (PADECO did a study on this aspect for OCMLT.)

5)   Organization of informal transports to provide complementary services to bus, boat, and rail transport systems.

6)   Improvement of physical facilities at the transfer points between bus routes and development/improvement of interchange facilities especially between bus and rail transit systems.

7)   Coordination of public transport services provided by different operators.

V. RELATIONSHIP TO PREVIOUS/OTHER PLANS

There exists a popular demand to connect all piers with bus routes. It is also observed that piers with bus connections are more popular among the boat passengers. Some effort has been made in the past for the physical integration of bus and boat services in the area. However, there has not been any comprehensive approach involving all the authorities which control and provide the services.

Very recently, to increase patronage of the rail transit system, the private sector operator (BTS) has taken initiatives to organize free feeder bus services to and from some of the stations. Clearly, this testifies the necessity of integrating bus and rail services for the mutual benefit of patrons and operators. However, the BTS initiative falls short of a broad-based approach to integrate the existing bus services provided by public and private sector operators. Currently the BTS rail services can serve only a limited number of commuters and are basically limited to providing distributional services for casual movement within the inner core of the city. However, with the planned extension of the BTS network and completion of the MRTA system which is currently under construction, the utility of rail transit services to the commuters would be greatly enhanced, and a qualitative change in the pattern of demand for rail services is expected. As such, to exploit the full potential of the rail services in addressing the traffic problems, serious efforts need to be made for integration of bus and rail services.

VI. EXPECTED IMPACT AND RESULTS

1)   Increased utility and patronage of public transport services in the area.

2)   Enhanced public transport passenger convenience.

3)   Increased accessibility of the area by public transport.

4)   General improvement of traffic and environmental condition in the area.

VII. BENEFICIARY GROUPS

Major beneficiary groups of the plan include commuters, school children, public transport users, people of the area, and visitors to the area.

VIII. ACTIVITIES TO BE UNDERTAKEN

Direct Activities:

1) Identify boat piers that have no direct access to bus services and investigate the possibility of local reorganization of bus services to pass by those piers.
2) Restructure bus services to match the derived demand from linked boat passenger trips.
3) Improve and/or develop interchange facilities between bus and boat transport systems and undertake road improvement and other physical measures, if necessary, so that buses can call directly or close to boat piers.
4) Introduce new bus routes for movement within Rattanakosin and provide feeder services to the BTS rail system and to the MRTA system (see also Action Plan 03).
5) Improve and/or develop interchange facilities between bus and rail transit systems.
6) Identify transfer points between bus routes and develop/improve interchange facilities.
7) Undertake a study to introducing a common ticketing system for rail mass transit and feeder bus services.
8) Organize local informal modes of transport (samlor, silor, etc.) to provide feeder services to bus and boat transport.

Supporting/complementary activities:

Development of a cooperation mechanism between transport operators
Riverfront development

Successful examples/models:

There are different forms of integration. In its simplest form it means physical (or system) integration of different modes that enable smooth transfer of passengers from one mode to another but does not consider a coordinated scheduling of services and common ticketing. In its most advanced form, it includes all of these features. Many German cities have an integrated public transport system of the most advanced form. However, the common form of system integration can be found in any developed city. Singapore is a good example in the region.

IX. RESPONSIBLE AUTHORITY/GROUPS/ALLIANCES

Responsible Authority:

Bangkok Metropolitan Administration (BMA)
Bangkok Mass Transit Authority (BMTA)
Department of Land Transport
Bangkok Transit System (BTS)
Mass Rapid Transit Authority (MRTA)
Harbour Department
Boat companies

Alliances:

Commuters in Rattanakosin Area
Office of the Commission for the Management of Land Traffic (OCMLT)
Police Department

X. EXTERNAL FACTORS/CONSTRAINTS/PREREQUISITES

Many operators in the public and private sector provide transit services. Likewise, a number of authorities are responsible for providing, managing and maintaining the infrastructure. It is difficult to accomplish the task of integrating all public transport modes without introducing a coordination mechanism for actions by these different actors.

XI. MONITORING INDICATORS AND EVALUATION

Monitoring Indicators:

Travel time for linked trips involving two or more modes
Transfer time at the interchanges
Public transport ridership
Opinion of public transport users
Number of boat piers with direct access to bus services
Bus feeder services to the rail transit system(s)

Evaluation:

Evaluation can be made from changes in quantitative and qualitative values of the indicators.

XII. RELATIONSHIP TO OTHER PLANS

This plan has a strong relationship to various actions under Action Plans 03, 05, 06, and 11.

XIII. REQUIRED FURTHER STUDIES AND INVESTIGATIONS

1) Inventory of physical facilities at the existing and possible other locations of modal interchanges.
2) Investigation on required forms of cooperation between service operators.
3) Study on issuance of a common ticketing system for multiple modes.

XIV. STAKEHOLDERS' REFERENCE (FEW)

070506 Should have an integrated traffic system involving both land and water transportation.

090109 Set up a good public transport system and encourage people to use public transport because it is the most efficient way to solve the problem.

090116 Should have a multi-mode public transport system.

020202 Expand mass transportation system to cover all areas in Bangkok. Increase more variety of mass transportation system in the area.

010201 Propose to have a public tram car system.

070502 Improve and promote water transportation as an alternative way of commuting.

090111 Should have a new kind of mass transport system such as subway. In Germany, the subway system is very good and it is one of the solutions for public transport.

060204 Since the Rattanakosin Area is surrounded with waterways, water transportation should be developed and if it already exists, it should be improved. This will provide another transportation alternative for people.

REFERENCES

PADECO, 1996. *Project to Study the Public Transport System's Joint Administration/Services Systems*, Phase 1, Final Report, OCMLT, Bangkok, Thailand.

TRAFFIC RESTRAINT AND DEMAND MANAGEMENT

ACTION PLAN 05

I. TITLE OF THE ACTION PLAN

Traffic Restraint and Demand Management

II. BACKGROUND AND CURRENT SITUATION

Bangkok is heavily dependent on private cars. Compared to other Asian cities in the region, both the level of car ownership and car use are significantly higher and are still increasing at a fast rate. However, increases in the supply of sufficient road space have not been able to keep pace with the burgeoning demand resulting from ever increasing car use. As a result, the city has remained to be infamous for its severe traffic and related environmental problems since the early seventies. As it is a part of the inner city area, the situation in Rattanakosin is worse than the average condition of the city.

In the past, commendable efforts have been made to address the city's transport problems, which have led to some improvement of the situation. Up until now, the main thrust of all such efforts has centred around searching for a solution to the problems from the supply side. A large number of road infrastructure projects of all descriptions and sizes have been implemented. Despite such efforts, Bangkok still enjoys much less road space in terms of road (to total area) ratio and network density compared with Tokyo, London, Singapore, or New York (JICA, 1997).

In recent times, there has been a realization that the elusive search for a supply side solution must be complemented by drastic demand side measures as well. However, it is important to mention here that the necessity of demand management measures has arisen largely due to the current imperfect system of transport pricing. In the present environment, prices have not reflected the cost of provision of the transport services and facilities. Consequently, this has lead to: waste of resources, insufficient funds to develop and maintain infrastructure, distortions in modal choice, and externalities (pollution and congestion). If an efficient pricing system can be introduced which is able to realize the full cost of travel from the users of transport services and facilities, the necessity of demand management measures may not exist at all. Until that time, it is important to consider restraint and demand measures. The popularly known MIT study of 1996 indicated that in order to manage traffic effectively, traffic flows had to be reduced by 30per cent of the levels of that year.

Realising the importance of restraint and demand management measures, OCMLT considered drastic measures including the introduction of an area licensing system, and an alternate day licence plate restriction scheme. However, the consideration of such measures came from a professional point of view and did not have popular support. As a result, they were never implemented. If any drastic measure like these are to receive essential political support, they must be fair, sustainable, and most importantly, all concerned stakeholders must be directly involved in the decision making process. Furthermore, viable alternatives to using a car must also be in place. Only then do drastic measures have a fair chance for their implementation.

The importance of traffic restraint and demand management measures appears to be well supported by the stakeholders of this planning exercise. In this respect, they suggested measures such as, "Decrease car volume using car-pool or using road pricing in rush hours as in Singapore"; and "Should not allow private cars with single occupants into the area". They even proposed more drastic actions such as, "Rattanakosin area should be a car-free area".

In many respects, car dependency has been described as a psychological problem by researchers. As such, the start of any solution has to be the promotion of the growing awareness that things could be better if there were fewer cars around or if ordinary everyday journeys could be made by alternatives to the car. As a part of any drastic traffic restraint and demand management program, first a public campaign needs to be made similar to the European car-free day of 22nd September as well as other actions.

III. MAJOR ISSUES AND PROBLEMS

1) High levels of traffic congestion and long delays.
2) High cost of transportation.
3) Severe air and noise pollution.
4) Increased requirements of fossil fuel.
5) High traffic safety hazards.
6) Deterioration in overall quality of life and high level of health hazards.
7) Unfriendly environment for pedestrian and community activities.
8) Demand for resources to create new infrastructure to accommodate the ever increasing volume of private transport.

IV. PROPOSED ACTIONS

1) Launching a public campaign to win wide support and participation of car owners to the introduction of traffic restraint and demand management measures.
2) Undertaking an evaluation of effectiveness of alternative measures for traffic restraint.
3) Conducting a study to introduce an area licensing scheme for the inner circle of Rattanakosin.
4) Restriction on low occupancy private cars in the area.
5) Introduction of demand management measures by staggering working hours of the government agencies in the area, promotion of car-pooling and operating staff buses.
6) Rationalization of the freight distribution system to minimize the volume of goods traffic in the area.

V. RELATIONSHIP TO PREVIOUS PLANS

The MIT consulting team study of 1996, the JICA plan on urban traffic in 1997, and OCMLT strongly advocated in favour of introducing demand management and traffic restraint measures. Based on the recommendations of a working committee in 1993, OCMLT decided to implement 17 management measures some of which were related to traffic restraint and demand management[1]. These measures included staggering of working hours, area licensing, and restrictions on private car use.

VI. EXPECTED IMPACT AND RESULTS

1) Reduced levels of traffic congestion and delays.
2) Reduced cost of public transport operation.
3) Improved level of service by public transportation.
4) Reduced negative impacts on environment.
5) Improved quality of life and reduced respiratory and other health hazards.
6) Enhanced pedestrian and community activities.
7) Reduced demand for fuel and resources to create new infrastructure.

VII. BENEFICIARY GROUPS

All road users and people living and working in the area will benefit from the plan. Because of the expected improvement in public transport operation due to reduced levels of congestion, both the passengers and operators would benefit. Indirectly, people of the whole country would also benefit because of lesser demand for financial resources to build new infrastructure and import fuel. The money could be used for other pressing needs.

VIII. ACTIVITIES TO BE UNDERTAKEN

Direct activities:

1) To start with, campaign for a car-free day early next year and then increase to 2-4 car-free days from a year after.
2) Conduct a study to introduce an area licensing scheme for the inner circle of Rattanakosin.
3) Introduce a "3-in-1" car travel scheme for through traffic passing through the area, particularly in the rush hours.
4) Promote car-pooling in big offices by linking it directly to parking policy.
5) Stagger the working hours in government offices in the area.
6) Subject to further study restrict private cars on selected roads to support pedestrian activities (refer to Action Plan 02).
7) Enforce parking control and management (refer to Action Plan 06).
8) Impose condition of having a garage for buying new cars (in Bangkok).
9) Restrict access to commercial/delivery vehicles during daytime.
10) Promote logistics services to make goods movement and distribution more efficient through joint delivery and disposal systems, preferably at night.

---

[1] The 17 measures include: enforcement of bus lanes; promotion of public transport systems; promotion of school bus services; staggering working hours in government offices; construction of suburban truck terminals; promotion of staff bus services; promotion of using taxis; strict enforcement of parking prohibitions; introduction of third party insurance; inspection of car engine before annual tax payment; increase of parking fees; revision of annual tax structure for car usage; promotion of "park and ride" facilities; strict truck ban in daytime; area licensing; various restrictions on private car use; and establishment of a transport fund from oil taxes.

Supporting/complementary activities:

Limiting of parking facilities and converting free parking to pay parking
Improvement of public transport
Marketing of transport demand management

Successful examples/model:

Almost all major cities in Europe and Asia apply some kind of restriction on private car use. An area licensing scheme has been in successful operation in Singapore since 1975. Manila introduced restriction on private cars one day a week based on the last digit of the licence plate number. This restriction has been in operation since 1996. Jakarta applies a "3-in-1" measure by prohibiting cars with less than 3 passengers on two main roads between 6 and 10 in the morning.

Last year Bangkok joined the club of cities of car-free day of 22nd September. Promoted by civil society groups and supported by the public leaders, the voluntary car-free day received encouraging response from the car owners. However, this should be borne in mind that voluntary schemes rely on socially responsible members of community and as such have limitations. These schemes may only be used to increase the level of public awareness regarding some problem(s) and not as their solutions.

IX. RESPONSIBLE AUTHORITY/GROUPS/ALLIANCES

Responsible Groups/Authority:

Office of the Commission for the Management of Land Traffic (OCMLT)
Bangkok Metropolitan Administration (BMA)
Government Departments located in the area
Local communities
Police Department

Alliances:

Academics and transport research institutions
Department of Town and City Planning
Department of Highway
Logistics service companies (Freight transport service providers)

X. EXTERNAL FACTORS/CONSTRAINTS/PREREQUISITES

Most of the measures under this plan have to be considered for the city as a whole as they cannot be considered for Rattanakosin in isolation. Improvement of the public transport system and winning a broad-based support of car owners and residents of the area are two major prerequisites. As the success of the plan depends heavily on parking control and management, parking policy needs to be well articulated with the actions under this plan.

XI. MONITORING AND EVALUATION

Monitoring indicators:

Volume of traffic
Average speed and delays
Average occupancy of private cars
Number people in car-pooling programmes
Improvement in travel time of bus transport
Traffic volume on car-free days
Car park occupancy
Compliance of restriction measures imposed
Increase in joint delivery and disposal of goods (in the supply chain)

Evaluation:

The success of the plan can be evaluated directly from the changes in quantitative values of the monitoring indicators. Periodic traffic surveys would be required to obtain the values of the monitoring indicators. An ex-post evaluation of traffic restriction measures should also be undertaken to judge their effectiveness.

XII. RELATIONSHIP TO OTHER PLANS

The traffic restraint and demand management plan has strong relationships to various actions under Action Plans 01, 03, 04, 06, 07, 11 and 12. The overall relationship is shown in Table 2.

XIII. REQUIRED FURTHER STUDIES

Promotion of car-pooling and other demand management measures
Study on introduction of an area licensing scheme
Effectiveness of alternative restraint measures for private cars
Logistics for the movement and distribution of goods

XIV. STAKEHOLDERS' REFERENCES (FEW EXAMPLES)

70504	Should not allow private cars with single occupants in the area.
010201	Reduce number of cars in the Rattanakosin area by using other alternative routes.
060116	Organize traffic system suitable for the area and prohibit trucks and tour buses.
070604	Forbid the entry of some specific types of vehicles e.g. the lorry, ten wheelers.
070508	Limit private cars and tour buses into the Rattanakosin area.
140101	Private cars except government vehicles should be charged.
070601	The Rattanakosin area should be a car-free area.
040104	Regulate and control the number of cars, not only trucks, which come into the Rattanakosin area.
021501	Use odd-even date system restricting cars coming into the area.
021602	Reduce the number of cars by restricting the age of drivers and cars, e.g. if the car

	is more than 10 years old, it should not be allowed in this area.
021801	If travelling a short distance, one should use public transportation.
021802	Use private car only when necessary.
030104	People who do not need to come into Rattanakosin Island should find other ways to transit the area. Traffic congestion would be reduced.
110101	Decrease car volume using car-pool (4 people) or using road pricing in rush hours as in Singapore.
150109	If possible in the future private cars should not be allowed in the area, only public transportation since it is an important tourist attraction. Roads should not have too many cars.
080103	Reduce the number of motorcycles in order to maintain order in the traffic system since they are more in number than cars and create more pollution.
120108	Enact a law for controlling the number cars in each house.
E100101	People who do not have a garage should not be allowed to own a car.

REFERENCES

Bangkok Metropolitan Authority, 1996. The Bangkok Plan: A Vision for Bangkok Metropolitan Administration Area, 1995-2005, prepared through a collaborative effort of the BMA Department of City Planning, the MIT Consulting Team, and the EC/BMA Project Team, Bangkok.

Japan International Cooperation Agency, 1997. *Final Report on Technical Assistance for Urban Traffic and Transport Planning,* prepared for The Office of the Commission for the Management of Land Traffic, Bangkok, Thailand.

COMPREHENSIVE
PARKING POLICY

ACTION PLAN 06

I. TITLE OF THE ACTION PLAN

Comprehensive Parking Policy

II. BACKGROUND AND CURRENT SITUATION

The problem of parking is quite widespread in Rattanakosin. The stakeholders identified it as one of the major problems in the area. Only a limited number of on- and off-street parking facilities are available for the residents and visitors to the area. As a result, very often drivers park illegally along the congested streets, which aggravates the congestion problem in the area. The parking problem is quite severe particularly around the schools and places of tourist attractions. Failing to get a parking space, many parent drivers simply cruise around the area in the afternoon peak hours until they can pick-up their child. This wasteful cruising adds further to the congestion problem of the area.

The area attracts a large number of local and foreign tourists everyday, many of whom come by special tourist buses. These tourist buses create serious parking problems particularly in areas surrounding the Grand Palace. The buses are parked on the streets for long hours, which affects traffic circulation of the whole area.

However, the apparent shortage of parking spaces may not be solved through direct supply of additional spaces as this can aggravate the overall traffic situation by attracting additional private cars in the area. In fact some of the stakeholders have suggested limiting the available parking spaces to relieve congestion problems. Any real demand for additional spaces needs to be carefully examined against alternative options available.

III. MAJOR ISSUES AND PROBLEMS

1) Traffic congestion due to on-street legal and illegal parking of private cars and tourist buses.
2) High incidence of illegal parking.
3) Invasion of pedestrian and public areas by parked vehicles.
4) Inadequacy of parking facilities for visitors and people who commute to the area.

IV. PROPOSED ACTIONS

1) Development of a comprehensive parking policy and management plan for the whole area as an integral part of local transport policy, other actions for the area, and within the strategic transport planning framework for the whole city, and paying special attention to parking needs of the residents and visitors.
2) Conducting a study to assess the parking needs in the area and alternative policy options available.
3) Identification of streets and other vacant/unused spaces which are suitable for parking.

4)   Introduction of a pricing system and other control measures especially to discourage/restrict long-term parking and to ensure continuous turnover of parking spaces for the visitors.

5)   Building of car parks/park and ride facilities outside Rattanakosin Area which can be used as transfer points or interchanges between private car and public transport.

6)   Construction of a limited number of off-street parking facilities to relieve localized parking problems with due attention to parking policy so that the new facilities do not invite additional traffic in the area. Parking incentives may be considered for those who are members of car-pooling clubs. Subject to further study the locations for new facilities can be near the giant swing and Sanam Luang. Such new facilities should only be considered when no other options are feasible or sufficient.

7)   Enforcement of parking control and management with the involvement of local volunteer traffic wardens, and using proper markings, signage, and mechanical devices.

8)   Promotion of the parking management plan through public campaign and support from the local community.

V. RELATIONSHIP TO PREVIOUS PLANS

The popularly known MIT Study of 1996 observed that a high level of car parking, particularly within the CBD encourages car use. The study recommended a policy of reducing the easy availability of parking in the inner city and suggested a revision of the standards imposed under Ministerial Regulation 7, 1974. It also proposed the reduction of existing facilities and converting free parking to pay parking. The JICA study (1997) also recommended a control on supply of parking facilities and introduction of pricing for on-street facilities.

VI. EXPECTED IMPACT AND RESULTS

1)   Reduced number of vehicles entering into Rattanakosin
2)   Improved traffic circulation and operation of public transport in Rattanakosin area.
3)   Increased accessibility of the area.
4)   Reduced incidence of illegal parking.
5)   Improved environment.
6)   Improved safety.
7)   Generation of revenue from parking charges.

VII. BENEFICIARY GROUPS

The major beneficiaries would include local residents, people who work in the area, and all road users. Public transport users, particularly commuters and school children, are also expected to benefit because of reduced traffic congestion and improved operation of buses and other public transport modes.

VIII. ACTIVITIES TO BE UNDERTAKEN

Direct Activities:

1) Select suitable sites to build off-street parking facilities for tourist buses and "park and ride" lots outside Rattanakosin.
2) Identify sites suitable for kerb-side parking and design appropriate parking bays considering road geometry, available space, safety hazard, and access to premises including access for loading and unloading.
3) Limit/restrict parking on all major roads according to a road classification system (as proposed in Action Plan 01).
4) Build limited number of off-street parking facilities at suggested and feasible locations.
5) Restrict parking of loading and unloading vehicles along streets with commercial premises to specified hours only.
6) Mark and sign all parking facilities and areas where parking is prohibited.
7) Introduce a pricing system and install mechanical devices for collection of parking charges.
8) Train and engage community traffic wardens to police parking infringements.
9) Install devices to deter illegal parking in restricted areas.
10) Designate parking areas for taxis close to places of tourist attractions, other places of interest, and major traffic generators.

Supporting/complementary activities:

A review of the parking standards imposed under Ministerial Regulation 7, 1974.
Enactment of legislation to allow community traffic wardens.
Preparation of training materials for community traffic wardens.
Promotion of car-pooling clubs in big offices.
Promotion of "park and ride" facilities

Successful examples/models:

In this region, Singapore has a successful parking management and control system in operation. Many major cities in the world have comprehensive parking policies for their central and other sensitive areas. In those cities, parking policies have been introduced as a part of a comprehensive transport policy and are integrated with actions involving improvement of public transport and traffic restraint measures.

IX. RESPONSIBLE AUTHORITY/GROUPS/ALLIANCES

Responsible authority/groups:

Bangkok Metropolitan Authority (BMA)
Bangkok Mass Transit Authority (BMTA)
Police Department
Local communities
Government Offices

Alliances:

Department of Town and City Planning
Office of the Commission for the Management of Land Traffic (OCMLT)
Tourism Authority of Thailand
Tour operators
Taxi and tuk-tuk operator's associations

X. EXTERNAL FACTORS, CONSTRAINTS, AND PREREQUISITES

Finding suitable space for developing park-and-ride facilities and other parking needs outside Rattanakosin is a crucial factor for this plan. As most of the parking facilities are privately owned, cooperation from local residents, business owners, tour operators, major employers and government offices in the area is an important factor for success of the plan. A revision of parking standards would also be helpful for a long-term effective solution of the problem.

XI. MONITORING AND EVALUATION

Monitoring indicators:

Number of illegal parking incidences
Average duration of on-street parking
Number of long-term parking
Rate of occupancy of car parks in the area
Utilization of "park and ride" facilities
Average travel speed through the area

Evaluation:

The number of illegal parking incidences along the streets should gradually reduce while average travel speed and volume of traffic on roads with parking restrictions should increase. Periodic parking surveys (parking lots and on-street parking) would be required. Evidence of unserved parking demand from parking surveys would indicate whether any change in parking policy is needed.

XII. RELATIONSHIP TO OTHER PLANS

This plan has strong relationship to various actions under Action Plans 01, 02, 04, 05, 09, 10 and 11.

XIII. REQUIRED FURTHER STUDIES

Revision of parking standards
Detailed land use survey of the area
Inventory of road network

Parking demand survey
Pricing of parking facilities
The enforcement implications
Traffic engineering measures to facilitate safe access to planned/proposed off-street car parks

XIV. STAKEHOLDERS' REFERENCES (FEW EXAMPLES)

060307   Should strictly regulate car parking.

021303   Disorderly parking should be solved by traffic officers because it makes traffic congestion.

020802   Should survey temporary parking lots before building permanent ones.

022402   Provide parking space so that no parking is allowed along the road.

021404   Control taxis and public buses to park in an orderly manner.

021003   Parking should be prohibited in some areas to solve traffic problems. Parking along the street decreases the road surface [available for smooth traffic flow].

060106   Provide parking with a charge - people will be more happy and government can gain money.

060119   Parking for coaches should be on the Thonburi side [of the Chao Phraya River] and tourists should use ferries to come to the Pranakorn side.

070606   Limit parking space or limit odd or even days or no parking at all. Parking should be available for residents in the area.

100104   Provide parking outside Rattanakosin Island and provide shuttle buses inside the island.

100105   [Authorities should be] strict with parking along the footpath. Provide public parking zones and limit shopping area.

100108   Providing parking spaces, using park and ride method.

020501   Inadequate parking space at tourist attraction places.

020509   If parking lots are provided, people are willing to pay.

060208   Underground parking lots should be built at the Giant Swing and Sanam Luang.

080301   Inadequate parking areas since there are many visitors to this area such as government officers, tourists, etc.

02505   Want underground parking at Sanam Luang.

02507   Wish to utilize certain area of Sanam Luang as a temporary parking lot and also to collect parking fees so that tourist coaches can park and tourists need not walk long distances.

02508   Want BMA to arrange parking spaces for tourist coaches because there are a large number of coaches with no parking spaces.

021601   Construct the underground parking lot underneath Sanam Luang because a large number of tourists visit this area. Although BMA allows parking in some areas, they are too far and the tourists must walk across the street where they occasionally face traffic accidents. If BMA has no budget, then BMA should encourage the private sector to invest and collect parking fees as well as to utilize this area for other commercial activities such as selling souvenirs, foods, drinks, etc. Besides, Sanam Luang still remains for royal functions; people can enjoy it as their recreation place and unpleasant visual scenery does not occur.

REFERENCES

Bangkok Metropolitan Authority, 1996. *The Bangkok Plan: A Vision for Bangkok Metropolitan Administration Area*, 1995-2005, prepared through a collaborative effort of the BMA Department of City Planning, the MIT Consulting Team, and the EC/BMA Project Team, Bangkok.

Japan International Cooperation Agency, 1997. *Final Report on Technical Assistance for Urban Traffic and Transport Planning*, prepared for The Office of the Commission for the Management of Land Traffic, Bangkok, Thailand.

SCHOOL TRAVEL PLANS

ACTION PLAN 07

I. TITLE OF THE ACTION PLAN

School Travel Plans

II. BACKGROUND AND CURRENT SITUATION

The share of school trips was about 11per cent of trips by all modes per day by purpose in Bangkok in 1989. With an increase of about 200per cent in the number, school trips by 1995 would have accounted for about 19per cent of all trips, the majority of which were made during the morning and afternoon rush hours. Although reliable statistics are not available on the modal split of school trips, various estimates indicate that the share of private cars is much higher compared to any other major city in the region.

Although some schools in Bangkok have school buses, it is common that parents prefer to drive their children to-and-from schools. The main reasons for this preference are summarized as follows:

1) Inadequate public transportation system and unavailability of reliable school bus facilities.
2) Parents' concern about personal safety of their children.
3) Good quality schools are located in few areas only, Rattanakosin being one of these, and they attract car-owner parents from all over the city.
4) Parents' preference in accompanying their children to school.
5) Increased car ownership in the metropolitan area.
6) Increased traffic congestion and fears about road safety.

The high proportion of school trips made by car contributes significantly to traffic congestion in Bangkok. The problem is even more serious in Rattanakosin where a number of good schools are located, which draw students from all over the city. The reduction in the level of traffic congestion on school holidays clearly indicates the impact of schools. In many instances this has prompted the concerned authorities to declare special school holidays in order to hold special events like the IMF-World Bank annual meeting in 1992, the Asian Games in 1999, and the UNCTAD Meeting in 2000.

III. MAJOR ISSUES AND PROBLEMS

1) School trips made by private cars have a significant impact on traffic congestion and other related problems in Rattanakosin.
2) School trips create serious parking problems and local traffic congestion in school localities.
3) High cost of school travel
4) Lack of higher standard schools in other localities.
5) Improvement of the standards at schools.

IV. PROPOSED ACTIONS

1) Formation of travel committees comprising school authorities, teachers and parents in each school to plan and consider various alternative travel arrangements for the students from different localities.

2) Introduction of school buses in a comprehensive manner through partnership arrangements between service providers and school authorities, and with direct participation in planning and management by parents, teachers, and local communities.

3) Introduction of community organized and privately operated small vehicle school buses from distant communities.

4) Campaigning and motivation of parents living in the same locality for car-sharing by their children when traveling to school.

5) Identification of safe drop-off/pick-up points near schools so that congestion and parking problems in the school localities can be avoided.

6) Creation of pedestrian-friendly environment especially in school localities so that children living close by can walk safely to school.

7) Launching a public campaign to win support and participation of parents and local communities in preparing school travel plans.

8) Organization of training programs in schools on children's safety, and for local volunteer traffic wardens on traffic management and safety (also refer to Action Plan 09 and 10).

9) Consideration of shifting some prestigious schools out of the area.

10) Initiating a programme to improve the standards at all schools.

V. RELATIONSHIP TO PREVIOUS PLANS

OCMLT initiated a plan for introducing school buses in 1998. Although a rational solution to address many of the existing problems, this plan has not been very popular among the parents due primarily to their lack of confidence in the service operators to ensure safety of their children. A taxi company also tried to pursue parents to use their service for the safe and secured journey of their children to and from schools. However, it did not work due to various reasons.

The Ministry of Education initiated a policy to organize school districts in Bangkok. This policy required that children living in a defined district could only attend the local schools. One of the objectives was to reduce the number of school trips made by car and other motorized modes. The plan, however, could not be made effective because of resistance from the parents on the grounds that standards of schools in different localities varied widely, and so they would prefer to send their children to schools of higher standard even if located far away from their places of living. They also pointed out that arbitrary definition of service area may create a possible problem for the pupils living at the boundary of two districts. A school of a neighbouring district could be located just on the opposite side of the road while schools of the district of their residence are located far away.

VI. EXPECTED IMPACT AND RESULTS

1) Decrease in the number of school trips made by car and other motorized modes.
2) Reduced level of traffic congestion in general and particularly around the schools in Rattanakosin.
3) Decreased parking demand and problems of illegal parking.
4) Improved environmental quality in school districts and in Bangkok in general.
5) Increased levels of walking, cycling and use of public transport.
6) Reduced cost of schooling and more free time for parents and children.

VII. BENEFICIARY GROUPS

The parents, school children, and service providers are the direct beneficiaries of this action plan. Other road users and the society at large would gain benefits indirectly through reduced levels of traffic congestion and pollution, and creation of gainful employment in the transport sector. Benefits would also accrue to society because of reduced fuel consumption and lesser damage to environment.

VIII. ACTIVITIES TO BE UNDERTAKEN

Direct Activities:

1) Form travel committees in all schools with parents, teachers, service providers, community leaders, and authorities to a) prepare and implement school travel plans, and b) regulate the services that may be provided by public/private operators.
2) Organize training programmes for the travel committees on available options and preparation of school travel plans with direct participation of all stakeholders.
3) Promote partnerships between private/public service providers and school authorities to provide school bus services.
4) Campaign to popularise school bus schemes among the parents and to motivate them in car-sharing for children to school.
5) Initiate actions at community level for safe walking and cycling to schools by older children.
6) Create pedestrian friendly environment from drop-off/pick-up points to schools.

Supporting/complementary activities:

Parking restrictions and lower speed limits are to be implemented around school areas for safety reasons and to discourage car usage. For example, some cities in the U.K. are introducing 20 km/hr speed limit.

Successful examples/models:

The city of Bangkok itself has successful models of school bus operation. For example, all the international schools have a reliable school bus system operated by private sector operators. Many local schools have also school buses. What is needed to extend such systems to all schools and make available a variety of alternatives (not just standard buses, may include smaller vehicles such as vans) to travel by car that suit individual needs.

IX. RESPONSIBLE AUTHORITY/GROUPS/ALLIANCES

Responsible   Groups/Authority:

Schools in Rattanakosin
Parents and Teachers Associations of schools
School children
People in Rattanakosin
Bangkok Metropolitan Administration (BMA)
District Councils of Rattanakosin
Department of Secondary Education

Alliances:

Bangkok Mass Transit Authority (BMTA)
Bus companies/Taxi cooperatives
Department of Land Transport
CBOs

X. EXTERNAL FACTORS/CONSTRAINTS/PREREQUISITES

Gaining confidence of parents in school bus systems and winning their support would be crucial to make the programme a success.

XI. MONITORING INDICATORS AND EVALUATION

Monitoring Indicators:

Modal share of school trips for different modes
Number of schools with travel plans for the children
Number of children in car-sharing travel arrangements by parents
Change in attitude of parents towards school bus systems
Number of schools with safe drop-off/pick-up points
Proportion of children going to schools in their own localities

Evaluation:

The success of the plan can be judged from a shift of modal choice for car to other modes and positive changes in quantitative values of the other indicators.

XII. RELATIONSHIP TO OTHER PLANS

This plan has strong relationship to various actions under Action Plans 02, 05, 08, 09 and 12 (refer to Table 2).

XIII. REQUIRED FURTHER STUDIES AND INVESTIGATIONS ON

Surveys on travel characteristics of school children
O-D Survey of children and parents of children attending schools in Rattanakosin
Studies on modal shares, and pupils' and parents' attitude
Studies on standards at schools

XIV. STAKEHOLDERS' REFERENCES (FEW)

E100104   Good school buses should be arranged, then parents do not need to drive their own car.
030102, 060306 Traffic inconvenience during morning and evening especially in   front of Rachini School.
010205   Publicize cooperation among students and parents.
020503   Go by foot if it is not too far.
050104   Promote the awareness/consciousness of students to study near their houses to reduce traffic problems.

REFERENCES/OTHER STUDIES

Department of the Environment, Transport and the Regions, 1999. *School Travel Strategies and Plans: A Best Practice Guide for Local Authorities*, United Kingdom. (www.local_transport.gov.uk/schooltravel/bpgla/05.htm)

Japan International Cooperation Agency, 1997. *Final Report on Technical Assistance for Urban Traffic and Transport Planning,* prepared for The Office of the Commission for the Management of Land Traffic, Bangkok, Thailand.

Toshikazu Shimazaki, Kazunori Hokao and Shihana Sulaiha Mohamed, 1994. *Comparative Study on Transportation Modal Choice in Asian Countries*, Transportation Research Board Annual Meeting, National Research Council, Washington D.C.

TRAFFIC CALMING

ACTION PLAN 08

I. TITLE OF THE ACTION PLAN

Traffic Calming

II. BACKGROUND AND CURRENT SITUATION

The need for traffic calming is directly reflected in some of the statements of local residents - "If you want to protect the area then you must siphon off the through traffic"; or "Drivers drive too fast...". In fact these statements corroborate the essence of traffic calming which is the combination of mainly physical measures that reduce the negative effects of motor vehicle use, alter driver behaviour and improve conditions for non-motorized street users (Lockwood, 1997).   Traffic calming involves various physical measures such as changes in street alignment, installation of barriers, and other physical barriers to reduce traffic speed and/or reduce volume of through traffic in the interest of street safety, liveability and other public purposes.

The residents of Rattanakosin have a general complaint about an unfriendly and unattractive environment for pedestrians in the area, which has been discussed earlier (refer to Action Plan 01 and 02). Traffic calming can greatly enhance the attractiveness of the street environment and facilitate pedestrian, NMT, and transit use. Besides creating safe and attractive streets in the neighbourhood, it can also incorporate the preferences and requirements of the people living along the streets, and be complementary to its historic conservation. The four broad types of traffic calming measures and their uses are as follow:

- **Vertical deflections** (such as hump, speed-table, raised intersection, raised pavement, raised pedestrian crossing); **horizontal shifts** (such as single- or two-lane slow point, midblock island, traffic circle); and **roadway narrowings** are intended to reduce speed and enhance the street environment for non-motorists.

- **Closures** (diagonal diverters, half closures, full closures, and median barriers) are intended to reduce through traffic by obstructing traffic movements in one or more directions.

There is a need and considerable potential for introducing suitable traffic calming measures on different local streets and pedestrian priority areas in Rattanakosin to make the area more safe, liveable and attractive as a whole. However, there is no general prescription about the suitability of any particular calming measure. Selection of a particular type depends primarily on the purpose and site conditions.

III. MAJOR ISSUES AND PROBLEMS

1)   Traffic safety hazards and inconvenience to road users due to fast moving traffic on local streets.

2)   High negative effects of motor vehicles on the environment particularly in areas of pedestrian activity and residential neighbourhoods.

3) Unfriendly and unattractive environment for pedestrians and cyclists.

IV. PROPOSED ACTIONS

1) Development of design standards, warrants and guidelines on different calming measures for residential neighbourhood streets and other higher order roads. (Warrants are minimum requirements that should be met, in most cases, before a particular device is installed.)
2) Establishment of project selection procedures and public involvement to consider alternative proposals.
3) Initiation of a traffic calming programme on an area wide basis with consideration for a number of streets being treated at the same time.

V. RELATIONSHIP TO PREVIOUS PLANS

The common measures of traffic calming such as road humps and traffic circles are common in Bangkok. However, these measures came into existence as spot improvements and mostly responding to local residents requests for action. They do not follow any design standard or warrants and guidelines for their set up. It is understood as most of the previous plans were made for the city level, traffic calming measures which form a component of local area transport plan, did not come within the purview of these plans.

VI. EXPECTED IMPACT AND RESULTS

1) Increased safety and perception of safety for pedestrians and non-motorized transport users.
2) Increased walking and use of NMVs, which are sustainable modes of transportation.
3) Reduced negative effects (noise, vibration, pollution) of vehicular traffic on the environment.
4) Enhanced street environment incorporating the preferences and requirements of the local people.
5) Reduced collision frequency and severity.
6) Reduced need for police enforcement.
7) Reduced volume of through traffic on local streets.
8) Enhanced community interaction.
9) Complements conservation of historic sites.

VII. BENEFICIARY GROUPS

All residents, people working in the area, and visitors are expected to benefit from reduced traffic safety hazards and improved traffic circulation. However, pedestrians especially those with special needs such as children, the elderly, and people with disabilities and non-motorized transport users will benefit the most.

VIII. ACTIVITIES TO BE UNDERTAKEN

Direct Activities:

1) Commission a team of professionals to develop design standards, warrants and guidelines for different calming measures.
2) Establish procedures for project selection and public involvement. Consider public involvement beyond the traditional techniques, new techniques such as computer imaging, and design charrettes to help all participants visualise design alternatives and participate constructively in the process.
3) Form local level committees with representation from local residents from all walks of life as well as concerned officials to draw up plans for traffic calming measures on an area wide basis.
4) Implement the plan as part of an overall transportation plan for the area.

Supporting/complementary activities:

Implementation of a comprehensive traffic management plan for the whole area.

Successful examples/model:

Traffic calming of major roads has been common in Europe for over a decade and the process has now been institutionalized. Schalabbach (1997) claims that the first deliberate use of vertical speed devices was introduced in Dutch cities in the 1970s, which ultimately culminated in changes to traffic regulations and publication of the first European design standards for *woonerven*, or shared zones. In the recent years hundreds of active traffic calming programmes have been introduced in the U.S. and Canadian cities and in fact it is now one of the most credible issues in transport planning activities. Berkeley, Boulder, Brookline, Chicago, Columbus, Houston, Phoenix, Portland, Seattle, Toronto are among those cities which have implemented extensive traffic calming projects.

IX. RESPONSIBLE AUTHORITY/GROUPS/ALLIANCES

Responsible Groups/Authority:

Bangkok Metropolitan Administration (BMA)
Local communities
Police Department

Alliances:

Academics and transport research institutions
Department of Town and City Planning
Office of the Commission for the Management of Land Traffic (OCMLT)
Department of Highway

X. EXTERNAL FACTORS/CONSTRAINTS/PREREQUISITES

Developing design standards and warrants.

XI. MONITORING AND EVALUATION

Monitoring indicators:

Opinion of pedestrians, NMT users, and local residents
Traffic speed (before and after)
Volume of through traffic
Frequency of incidences

Evaluation:

The success of the plan can be judged directly from the public opinion and reduction in traffic speed and numbers of incidences and through traffic

XII. RELATIONSHIP TO OTHER PLANS

The success of the plan depends on the implementation of Acton Plan 01and has strong relationship to various actions under Action Plans 02 and 07 (refer to Table 2).

XIII. REQUIRED FURTHER STUDIES

Study on warrants for traffic calming measures
Development of design standards for different calming measures and associated street scaping
Effectiveness of existing measures

XIV. STAKEHOLDERS' REFERENCES (FEW EXAMPLES)

022001	Drivers drive too fast especially those public buses.
070604	To avoid entering in this area, the alternative shortcuts should be defined.
070606	Traffic management in Rattanakosin area should lead to a smooth flow and should not allow large vehicles entering in this area.
070504	Should not allow private cars with single occupants.
070602	Should find effective and sustainable solutions to traffic congestion.
080105	BMA should consider which road should have what kind of traffic.
140101	Do not allow vehicles of more than six wheels in this area.
080107	Trucks should not be allowed to pass through this area. Strict on exhaust emission control.
100113	If you want to protect the area then you must siphon off the through traffic.

REFERENCES

Lockwood, Ian, 1997. "ITE Traffic Calming Definition", *ITE Journal*, vol. 67, p. 22.

Schalabbach, K., 1997. "Traffic calming in Europe", *ITE Journal*, vol. 67, p. 22.

COMMUNITY TRAFFIC
WARDEN PROGRAMME

ACTION PLAN 09

I. TITLE OF THE ACTION PLAN

Community Traffic Warden Programme

II. BACKGROUND AND CURRENT SITUATION

The stakeholders expressed their views on enforcement problems of traffic regulations in Rattanakosin. In many cases they felt that the current problems have arisen due to insufficient positive guidance to traffic and poor enforcement of traffic regulation orders. They also felt that more effective enforcement of traffic regulation orders was necessary, particularly against illegal parking, intruders into bus lanes, control of particular turning movements, etc. They opined that traffic police should be more proactive in guiding traffic rather than "wasting their valuable time to monitor parking problems". There is, however, a shortage of adequate police manpower resources for effective enforcement of traffic regulations and to guide and control the flow of traffic.

As a part of an overall solution to a shortage of police manpower resources, it was suggested that a group of local citizens were willing to volunteer as traffic wardens. The traffic wardens could complement the local police to enforce traffic regulations. However, their duties should be limited to providing positive guidance to drivers and pedestrians, enforcement of regulations which are easy to execute, dealing with minor offences, and helping pedestrians, school children, the elderly, and people with disabilities. They may not be allowed, for example, to deal with complicated legal matters. Involvement of the local community in traffic management would also help increase public consciousness about traffic regulations.

There are two major issues in introducing a community traffic warden system in Rattanakosin. First, an implementation programme has to be drawn up with details on how the system should function. It should contain, inter alia, a charter of functions and duties of the wardens, a set-up for their functioning, and an institutional arrangement for working with the police. The second issue would involve recruitment of volunteers from the communities, and organizing training on traffic laws and regulations, help to pedestrians and drivers, and personal and traffic safety hazards.

III. MAJOR ISSUES AND PROBLEMS

1) High incidence of traffic rule violation by road users.
2) The need for positive guidance to drivers especially about parking.
3) Illegal parking on the streets.
4) Traffic safety problems.
5) Violation of traffic signals and signs.
6) Lack of pedestrian support patrols to help school children, the elderly, and people with disabilities in crossing streets, guiding tourists to their places of interest, controlling of pedestrian movement along busy traffic routes, and for other purposes.
7) Personal security concerns.

IV. PROPOSED ACTIONS

1) Institutionalization of a community traffic warden system within the present organizational arrangements for traffic management.
2) Publicity of the community traffic warden programme in the media and local communities, and creation of public awareness about traffic rules and regulations.
3) Preparation of a detailed programme about organizational arrangements, logistics aspects, charter of duties and rules for the community wardens
4) Development of partnerships with local communities, CBOs, police department, and school authorities for implementation of the plan.
5) Organization of training programmes for the volunteer wardens on traffic laws and regulations, help to pedestrians and drivers, personal and traffic safety hazards, and rules related to their functions.

V. RELATIONSHIP TO PREVIOUS PLANS

This is a new plan. Although indications were given in some earlier plans, no specific measures were suggested.

VI. EXPECTED IMPACT AND RESULTS

1) Enhanced enforcement of traffic regulations.
2) Reduced illegal parking.
3) Improved traffic discipline in general in the area.
4) Reduced localized traffic congestion.
5) Improved perception of safety from traffic hazards particularly for school children and other disadvantaged groups.
6) Increased level of personal security.
7) Increased public awareness about traffic regulations.

VII. BENEFICIARY GROUPS

Direct beneficiaries are the communities at large, school children, pedestrians, cyclists and people with special needs.

VIII. ACTIVITIES TO BE UNDERTAKEN

Direct Activities:

1) Publicize the plan widely to win direct support of the community, local NGOs and CBOs for its implementation in the area.
2) Decide on functions, responsibilities, and training needs of the community traffic wardens through a participatory approach involving the residents, prospective volunteers, Police Department, and CBOs.
3) Prepare training materials, instruction handouts, and secure logistics support

needed to implement the programme.

4) Select young people from local communities and schools who would be willing to volunteer as traffic wardens.

5) Organize training programmes in cooperation with the Police Department, and local NGOs and CBOs.

6) Prepare an implementation scheme for the plan.

7) Start the programme after wide publicity in the area and media.

Supportive/complementing activities:

Programmes to create public awareness about traffic regulations and provide help to pedestrians

Successful examples /models:

A Traffic Warden Scheme was introduced in London in 1960 initially to enforce parking regulations. Subsequently, they have been assigned to other responsibilities such as, traffic control, issuance of penalty notices for traffic violations, etc. However, they are not volunteers. A citizen traffic warden scheme was introduced in New Delhi in 1997. The wardens have special training on road safety and they participate effectively in traffic management of the city. Volunteer school crossing patrols to help pedestrian school children are common in the United States of America.

IX. RESPONSIBLE AUTHORITY/GROUPS/ALLIANCES

Responsible Authority:

Local community and community based organizations (CBOs)
Police Department
Department of Land Transport
District Councils
Bangkok Metropolitan Administration

Alliances:

Office of the Commission for the Management of Land Traffic (OCMLT)
Department of Secondary Education
School authorities

X. EXTERNAL FACTORS/CONSTRAINTS/PREREQUISITES

Local traffic wardens are proposed to be engaged on a voluntary basis. Therefore the programme needs strong community support and motivation to induce young people to work as traffic wardens. Direct cooperation from the Police Department would be needed to launch the programme and introduce short training courses for the wardens.

XI. MONITORING AND EVALUATION

Monitoring indicators:

Number of volunteers trained and engaged
Periodic survey of illegal parking and number of tickets issued
Incidence of traffic rule violations
Number of accidents with pedestrian involvement
Opinion of local residents and school children

Evaluation:

The success of the plan can be judged from decreasing number of traffic incidences, reducing occurrence of traffic rule violations, and public opinion.

XII. RELATIONSHIP TO OTHER PLANS

This Plan has strong relationship to Action Plans 02, 06, 07, 10 and 12.

XIII. REQUIRED FURTHER STUDIES

Organizational arrangements for the programme
Assessment of training needs

XIV. STAKEHOLDERS' REFERENCES (FEW EXAMPLES)

021303   Disorderly parking should be solved by traffic officers because it makes traffic congestion.
100102   Make people more conscious about traffic regulations.
020501   [Want] to be a local guide and think of Rattanakosin Island promotion to the public.
022707   Make known and promote traffic law and information. It will alleviate traffic problem.
030401   Provide a team of officers (4-5 persons) to monitor traffic order in order to reduce accident and be strict on traffic discipline.

CORRECTION OF POOR ROAD USING HABITS

ACTION PLAN 10

I. TITLE OF THE ACTION PLAN

Correction of Poor Road Using Habits

II. BACKGROUND AND CURRENT SITUATION

The people of Rattanakosin have a major concern about poor road using habits in the area. As mentioned by many of them "Drivers have no traffic discipline"; "Bus drivers in the Rattanakosin area have poor driving manners ...which is the main cause of accidents"; or "Educate people on how to use cars and roads". However, one should not get the impression from these citations that the problem of poor road using habits is unique to Rattanakosin. This is a common problem in Bangkok. The residents of the area have a general complaint against poor, uncourteous and reckless driving, particularly by bus drivers, and yet again by the green minibus drivers.

It has been observed that people from all sections of the road users, including drivers, pedestrians, school children, vendors, and others are not always interested about following traffic discipline at intersections, pedestrian crossings, pedestrian areas, parking areas, and other public areas. Enforcement of traffic regulations is not always very satisfactory for various reasons. Violators of traffic regulations are not often apprehended. Yet again, if caught violators only have to pay a nominal fine for traffic offences. As a result, frequent conflicts arise owing to violations of rules and regulations, and competing demands from various groups of road users, which in turn lead to traffic safety hazards, congestion, and other incidences. indifferent

The problems of poor road using habits, however, arise not always because of road users' sheer indifference to traffic discipline. As observed by many of the stakeholders, very often poor habits arise due to road users' lack of "consciousness and awareness about traffic regulations" and problems of their attitude to other users. Simple punitive financial actions against the violators cannot be remedies to these more fundamental causes. Furthermore, not all types of bad road using behaviours can be controlled by regulations anyway. Regulations themselves are also subject to limitations due to enforcement and other problems.

An alternative to correction of poor road using habits could be to bring changes in the attitude of road users to fellow users by raising their awareness about traffic discipline and manners through a broad-based public campaign and community driven programmes to "train people to be disciplined with traffic regulation". Rather than imposing fines, road users with poor habits could be compelled to attend training courses and participate in traffic related community activities for correction of their habits. For example, drivers with poor driving habits could be required to watch videotapes of proper driving manners, learn all regulations regarding proper driving, etc. Incentives for good driving manners of bus drivers and harsh fines for repeated habitual violators may also be considered to complement the correction measures.

III. MAJOR ISSUES AND PROBLEMS

The major problems created in the area by poor road using habits are as follows:

1) Confusion and conflicts in road use.
2) Traffic safety hazards and inconvenience to road users.
3) Increased number of traffic incidences.
4) Unnecessary traffic congestion and related problems therefrom.
5) Unfriendly environment for pedestrians and cyclists.
6) Difficulties in fast movement of emergency vehicles.
7) Inconvenience in using the road by people with special needs such as children, sick people, elderly and people with disabilities.

IV. PROPOSED ACTIONS

1) Launching a public campaign highlighting the importance of good road using habits, manners, and the responsibilities of different road users.
2) Forming partnerships and alliances with the concerned stakeholders for the correction of identified poor habits.
3) Organization of appropriate training programmes for different groups of road users with direct participation of the stakeholders.
4) Introduction of course materials on good road using manners and habits, and traffic safety in the school curricula.
5) Enforcement of corrective/punitive measures for poor road using habits and for the violators of traffic discipline.

V. RELATIONSHIP TO PREVIOUS PLANS

This is a new plan.

VI. EXPECTED IMPACT AND RESULTS

1) Improved traffic circulation in the area in general.
2) Reduced traffic safety hazards, and improved perception of safety for walking particularly by disadvantaged groups, and users of non-motorized transport.
3) Enhanced image of public transport (bus transport in particular)
4) Reduced need for enforcement by police/traffic warden.
5) Increased motivation for using non-motorized modes of transportation for short distance trips due to reduced traffic safety hazards and improved perception of safety.

VII. BENEFICIARY GROUPS

All road users in the area are expected to benefit from reduced traffic safety hazards and improved traffic circulation. However, pedestrians especially those with special needs such as children, elderly, and people with disabilities and non-motorized transport users will benefit the most.

VIII. ACTIVITIES TO BE UNDERTAKEN

1) Form partnerships with local communities, community based organizations, BMTA, Police Department, and school authorities in the area to develop and implement various actions for correcting poor road using habits.
2) Identify the poor habits of major concern and the type of training or other activities, actions, and means necessary for their correction with direct participation of all stakeholders, professionals and academics.
3) Prepare training materials for the improvement of road using habits of different road users such as, school children, car drivers, drivers of public transport, and other groups with the participation of parents, local residents, school authorities, CBOs, BMTA, and Police Department.
4) Start appropriate training programmes for different groups.
5) Enforce corrective/punitive measures for poor road using habits which may include compulsory attendance of correction classes.
6) Provide incentives to public transport drivers for good road using habits
7) Develop a database of violators.
8) Launch a public campaign to increase general awareness about good road sing habits.

Supporting/complementary activities:

A regular driver training programme on good road using habits and manners by BMTA and other private operators is required. BMTA may consider organization of such training programmes by private operators as a condition to franchising.

Successful examples/model:

In Japan, children learn about good road using habits and manners at school as a part of the curricula. In many countries, besides testing of driving skills and rules, road behaviours are also observed/tested before granting a driving licence.

IX. RESPONSIBLE AUTHORITY/GROUPS/ALLIANCES

Responsible Authority:

Police Department
Bangkok Metropolitan Administration (BMA)
Bangkok Mass Transit Authority (BMTA)
District Councils
Private bus companies
School authorities

Alliances:

Community organizations

Office of the Commission for the Management of Land Traffic (OCMLT)
Department of Land Transport
Academics (including psychologists and sociologists)

X. EXTERNAL FACTORS/CONSTRAINTS/PREREQUISITES

This is a new scheme and its success would be dependent upon active cooperation of all stakeholders. Changes in people's attitude to fellow road users are the prime concern of this plan. However, any significant change in people's attitudes and its reflection in their behaviour may not be expected overnight. It may take a long time before the benefits of the plan can be noticed and appreciated.

XI. MONITORING AND EVALUATION

Monitoring indicators:

Number of violators in Rattanakosin
Number of repeating violators
Number of traffic incidences due to bad road behaviour
Change in road users' attitude, behaviour, and public opinion

Evaluation:

The general success of the plan can be measured by considering people's opinion (qualitative) about changes in poor road using habits, by conducting traffic surveys to observe road users' behaviour, and from positive changes in the values of the indicators.

XII. RELATIONSHIP TO OTHER PLANS

This plan has strong relationships to various activities under Action Plans 06, 09, and 12.

XIII. REQUIRED FURTHER STUDIES

Assessment of training needs or other suitable activities necessary for correction of poor road using habits of different groups of road users.

Study on motivation of bus drivers and incentives for good road manners.

XIV. STAKEHOLDERS' REFERENCES (FEW EXAMPLES)

080106   Mass transit buses are very undisciplined especially those minibus drivers who are so rude and wicked.

020202   The drivers of mass transport have bad behaviour and buses are not in a good condition.

070306   Drivers have poor manners and do not respect any regulations.
050105   Train people to promote consciousness and awareness on traffic regulations.
040205   Provide knowledge and PR to public about the rules and regulations.
100102   Make people more conscious about traffic regulations.
030102   Train people to be disciplined in traffic regulations.
022707   Make known and promote traffic law information to alleviate traffic problems.
070203, 080205 Drivers have no respect for traffic disciplines.
021001, 100106, 100103 Drivers do not respect traffic regulations and traffic lights.
080103   Bus drivers in the Rattanakosin Area have poor driving manners especially the joint-service buses such as minibus which is the main cause of accidents.
022001   Drivers drive too fast especially those public buses.
021801   Drivers do not respect the traffic regulations such as not stopping at red traffic lights and causing accidents.
021801   Follow traffic law concerning crossing the road.
040504   Regulation for drivers and pedestrians.
010202   Educate people on how to use cars and roads.
060310   Long time plan should be education which promotes public consciousness in students about social responsibilities not only the law.
040207   Government agencies must educate people about traffic regulations. Traffic sign should be in good condition.
060113   Support people awareness concerning [traffic] discipline. Department of Education should formulate traffic discipline courses.
120108   Train drivers about traffic discipline in order to stimulate public conscious and make them respect the rules.
E200103 Public education is very important. There are many measures that could generate results rather quickly. For example, on the overpass bridges for pedestrians, lines have been drawn in the middle to separate people going in opposite directions. It helps a lot in moving people efficiently. Similar measures could be implemented to urge people to abide by the traffic rules and any other socially accepted norms.
E100205 People should be educated about the traffic rules and any other socially accepted behaviour.

COMMUTING FROM THE THONBURI SIDE OF THE CHAO PHRYA RIVER

ACTION PLAN 11

I. TITLE OF THE ACTION PLAN

Commuting from the Thonburi side of the Chao Phrya River

II. BACKGROUND AND CURRENT SITUATION

A large number of people commute everyday by their private cars from the Thonburi side of the Chao Phrya River to Bankok on the other side of the river. A large proportion of those commuters pass through Rattanakosin. The presence of a large volume of through traffic generated by the commuters makes the roads of the area congested, particularly those leading to the bridges. However, once congestion starts building up, it does not remain limited only to the roads leading to the bridges but eventually spreads out all over the area.

Currently there are eight bridges, which provide direct road transport linkages between the two sides of the river and one more is being constructed. Besides bridges, the express boat and ferry services also serve a limited portion of the demand for daily river crossings. Apparently, the limited number of bridges have capacity constraints and cannot handle the commuter traffic movement satisfactorily. The bridges and the road network in their vicinity remain heavily congested during the peak hours, and consequently the commuters and other road users are subject to long delays and other adverse impacts of congestion. Congestion on the bridges, particularly on the Phra Pin Klao Bridge, is believed to be a major cause of traffic problems in Rattanakosin. This has led to a popular demand for the construction of new bridges to facilitate fast river-crossings by the commuters.

However, the stakeholders have also mentioned, "Find the way to reduce the number of cars using Pin Klao Bridge". Construction of more bridges may actually aggravate the existing situation further due to limited capacity of the road network serving the bridges. The existing road network on the Bangkok side of the river is already overloaded. Therefore any proposal for a new bridge site needs to be carefully examined against the available network capacity. Any new bridge may require the addition of supplementary capacity to the existing road network in the vicinity of the bridge. In fact, this has been pointed out by several stakeholders. As an alternative to new bridge construction, which is time consuming and also questionable on effectiveness and sustainability grounds, efforts can be made to enhance the existing bridge capacities by technical and management measures. These measures can be implemented in the short term to bring relief to the existing problems and can also help reduce the negative impacts of traffic movement in the area as a whole.

It is important to emphasize that this approach addresses the bridge congestion problem itself and at the same time reduces the general traffic problem in the area. In contrast, creating additional bridge capacity through new construction may solve the bridge congestion problem but certainly will make the general traffic condition in Rattanakosin (or for that matter in Bangkok) worse unless it can be matched by enhanced capacity of the road network.

III. MAJOR ISSUES AND PROBLEMS

1) Lack of capacity of the road bridges providing direct linkage between Thonburi and Bangkok.
2) Traffic congestion on the roads in the vicinity of the bridges.
3) Spillover of private commuter cars to and from Thonburi on all roads of Rattanakosin.

IV. PROPOSED ACTIONS

1) Identification of the nature of the real problem by ascertaining to what extent the problems are caused due to capacity limitations of the bridges and to what extent due to capacity constraints of the road network serving the bridges.
2) Conducting a study to examine a) the possibility of enhancing the technical efficiency of the bridges, and b) the scope of applying demand management measures to reduce the volume of commuter vehicular traffic across the river, particularly private cars.
3) Determination of the extent to which the demand for cross Chao Phraya road commuter traffic can be reduced through improvements to ferry services and their integration with bus transport.

V. RELATIONSHIP TO PREVIOUS PLANS

There have been a number of plans to build new bridges across the Chao Phraya. Currently, one of these (the Rama VIII Bridge) is under construction.

VI. EXPECTED IMPACT AND RESULTS

1) Reduced congestion on the bridges and the road network in their vicinity.
2) Improved environment and reduced negative impacts of traffic.
3) Reduced cost of public transport operation and improved services.

VII. BENEFICIARY GROUPS

All road users and residents of Rattanakosin, commuters across the Chao Phraya, and public transport users are expected to benefit directly from this plan. In addition, due to reduced negative impacts of vehicular traffic, pedestrians especially those with special needs such as children, elderly, and people with disabilities and non-motorized transport users will also benefit.

VIII. ACTIVITIES TO BE UNDERTAKEN

Direct activities:

1) Determine if the full capacity of the bridges are being utilized.

2) Consider introducing reversible lanes on the bridges.

3) Introduce HOV (high occupancy vehicle) lanes on the bridges (a private car with three or more passengers may be considered as an HOV).

4) Introduce moderate pricing for bridge crossings during the peak hours with free HOV lanes.

5) Develop park-and-ride facilities on the Thonburi side and connect them by good quality bus services.

6) Identify the bottlenecks on the road network and determine how they can be addressed.

7) Prioritize movement (through signal priorities and traffic management measures) on the primary roads across the Chao Phraya River.

8) Improve ferry and boat services and integrate them with bus services (refer to Action Plan 04).

9) Review the available studies on new bridges and decide if any new bridges are required after undertaking the above activities.

10) If new bridges are still required, consider double decking of some existing bridges and then other new sites.

Supporting/complementary activities:

Enhancement of the capacity of roads leading directly to the bridges.

Successful examples /model

Enhancement of bridge and tunnel capacities through technical and management measures is widely practiced all over the world. The Liverpool-Birkenhead tunnels in the U.K. and San Francisco Bay Bridge in the U.S.A. are good examples of the application of technical and management measures to enhance capacity.

IX. RESPONSIBLE AUTHORITY/GROUPS/ALLIANCES

Responsible Groups/Authority:

Bangkok Metropolitan Administration (BMA)
Bangkok Mass transit Authority (BMTA)
Office of the Commission for the Management of Land Traffic (OCMLT)
Department of Highway
Police Department

Alliances:

Boat service operators
Local communities
Academics and transport research institutions
Department of Town and City Planning

X. EXTERNAL FACTORS/CONSTRAINTS/PREREQUISITES

Improvement of public transport services
Availability of space to develop park and ride facilities
Success of the application of demand management measures

XI. MONITORING AND EVALUATION

Monitoring indicators:

Volume of private commuter cars passing through the area
Average occupancy of private commuter cars
Level of congestion on the bridges and adjoining road networks
Utilization of the HOV lanes and park and ride facilities by private cars
Increases in the shares of commuter traffic by ferry and boat services
Number of commuters using public transport

Evaluation:

Evaluation can be done directly from the differences in the values of the monitoring indicators before and after implementation of the technical and management measures to enhance bridge capacities. These values should be collected on regular basis through standard traffic engineering surveys.

XII. RELATIONSHIP TO OTHER PLANS

This plan has strong relationships to various activities under Action Plans 01, 03, 04,05 and 06 (refer to Table 2).

XIII. REQUIRED FURTHER STUDIES

Study on demand for Commuting from the Thonburi side of the Chao Phrya River
Determination of capacities of the road bridges and the adjoining road network
Study to determine optimum bridge pricing to influence higher occupancy of private cars

XIV. STAKEHOLDERS' REFERENCES (FEW EXAMPLES)

040104   Ease traffic flow by moving the central market (Pak Klong Talaad) and government buildings (some or all) out of the area. Find the way to reduce the number of cars using Pin Klao Bridge. Hopefully the Rama VIII Bridge will help when it is finished.
040305   There should be another bridge connecting the two-sides of the Chao Phraya River.
060302   Build tunnel under the Chao Phraya River.

060203	Construct more roads and an additional bridge across the Chao Phraya River to ease the traffic condition in the Rattanakosin area.
020603	Build tunnel under the Chao Phraya River and allow only public transport to use it. Travel in Rattanakosin area by bikes, buses and by foot.
021802	Build more bridges to reduce car volume in and out of the area. Should have restricted time for cars coming in and out of the area. Build roads going round the island so that some cars will not have to come inside.
020101	Increase alternative ways for people to go to work without passing through this area.
E248206	I know that Rama VIII Bridge is being built and can relieve traffic a little. But not enough, more bridges need to be built.
E100112	Build more bridges across the Chao Phraya River to take traffic away from the Phra Pin Klao Bridge.

COLLECTIVE AND SHARED RESPONSIBILITY FOR THE DEVELOPMENT OF RATTANAKOSIN

ACTION PLAN 12

I. TITLE OF THE ACTION PLAN

Collective and Shared Responsibility for the Development of Rattanakosin

II. BACKGROUND AND CURRENT SITUATION

Many of the current traffic and transportation problems in Rattanakosin involve hard policy choices. Considering the limitations of the traditional "top-down" approach, the present planning exercise has followed a "bottom-up" participatory approach to win public support especially to deal with the questions of difficult policy choices and public actions. All action plans presented so far, reflect the views of the stakeholders and are duly based on their recommendations. The stakeholders participated directly to make their views known. However, in a participatory approach, the role of the participants is not limited to making their views known or to forwarding a few suggestions at the planning stage. They also have an active role in the implementation phase and are to be directly involved with the implementation of most of the action plans. Further, to extending essential support, their involvement in implementation may vary from an individual action concerning behavioural change to direct contribution and participation in some of the activities.

III. MAJOR ISSUES AND PROBLEMS

1)   People's support to public campaigns and required involvement in different activities.
2)   Collective and shared responsibility for development.
3)   Collaborative resolution of conflicts in interest.
4)   People's participation to implement the plans.

IV. PROPOSED ACTIONS

1)   Initiation of a public promotion programme to raise awareness about collective and shared responsibility for development and to involve all local residents in the implementation of the plans.
2)   Organization of citizens' forums at the street and community levels to discuss their own duties and responsibilities, and actions.
3)   Formation of liaison committees to coordinate their actions.

V. RELATIONSHIP TO PREVIOUS PLANS

This approach has not been tried in Bangkok or Thailand. However, as discussed in the first section of this report, participatory approaches in general have a firm standing within the broader contexts of constitutional provisions and the on-going reorganization of local government functions in Thailand. In the near future, changes are expected in functioning of the local governments at all levels to accommodate community participation.

VI. EXPECTED IMPACT AND RESULTS

1) Sustainable development of the area.
2) Enhanced community interaction and better understanding about the problems faced by different sections of the community and collaborative resolution of conflicts in interest.
3) Improved governance and self-determination.
4) Reduced requirement of resources for public agencies.
5) A model for sustainable urban development in Thailand and in the region.

VII. BENEFICIARY GROUPS

All road users and residents living in Rattanakosin will benefit directly and the people of Bangkok in general will also benefit indirectly.

VIII. ACTIVITIES TO BE UNDERTAKEN

1) Organize public promotion programmes as mentioned in different Action Plans.
2) Motivate people to support, join and participate in community activities.
3) Form citizens' forums and liaison committees at the street and community levels to debate various issues of concern and take decisions for actions.
4) Initiate activities by the citizens' forums to make people aware about collective and shared responsibility for development and motivating towards making behavioural change concerning (but not limited to):

    a.   Support and participation in community activities
    b.   Refraining from wrong/bad road using habits.
    c.   Patronizing use of public transport.
    d.   Limiting the use of private cars voluntarily.
    e.   Giving way to pedestrians and other people with special needs.
    f.   Honouring the rights of other road users.
    g.   Walking for short trips.
    h.   Teaching children about right road using habits and road manners.
    i.   Avoiding littering of public places or discharging waste water-to-water bodies.

Supporting/complementary activities:

Activities by CBOs and local NGOs to organize the communities.

Successful examples/model:

In the recent years, many interesting examples of partnerships with the community and civil society in planning, decision-making and management of local level affairs have emerged in Mexico, Peru, Columbia and other Latin American countries. Good practices of partnerships in local government exist in South Africa for the purposes of planning, local economic development, environmental management, waste disposal, etc. Urban communities in the U.S.A. and many European countries are also now taking greater interest in the affairs of their local governments. Different types of institutional arrangements have been devised to facilitate partnerships with the community and civil society. For example, Scottish Civic Forums have been established in Scotland. The forum is a place where members of the civil society and community groups debate various issues of concern and take decisions for actions. There are also good examples of people's participation and contribution in planning and management of urban services/facilities at the community level in the City of Bangkok, some of which have already been mentioned in Part I of this report.

IX. RESPONSIBLE AUTHORITY/GROUPS/ALLIANCES

Responsible Groups/Authority:

Local communities
CBOs and NGOs
Bangkok Metropolitan Administration (BMA)
District offices of BMA

Alliances:

Office of the Commission for the Management of Land Traffic (OCMLT)
Police Department

X. EXTERNAL FACTORS/CONSTRAINTS/PREREQUISITES

People's conviction about collective and shared responsibility for development and willingness to support, join and participate in community activities

XI. MONITORING AND EVALUATION

Monitoring indicators:

Number of citizens' forums formed
Proportion of people aware about their collective and shared responsibilities
Degree of involvement of local residents in implementation of the plans
Changes in attitude and behaviour of people

Evaluation:

Social and other surveys are to be undertaken to observe and monitor people's involvement in implementation, and changes in their attitudes and behaviours. An increase in people's involvement and positive changes in their observed behaviour can be considered as evaluation criteria for success.

XII. RELATIONSHIP TO OTHER PLANS

This plan is related to almost all other action plans.

XIII. REQUIRED FURTHER STUDIES

Methods of effective participation in community activities
Identification of collective and shared responsibilities for development
Benchmark surveys regarding people's road using behaviour
Motivating people to behavioural changes

XIV. STAKEHOLDERS' REFERENCES (FEW EXAMPLES)

060116   Community participation is necessary.
040402   Work plans should include forums to have public opinions before implementation, since they will be sounding boards of the communities to voice about the projects.
060202   Support community self-administration such as Phra Arthit community to organize their own affairs.
010405   Willing to participate in every project as planner, activist, mediator, creator, presenter, and to establish a foundation to raise funds from foreign corporations and to manage human resources.
070310   Houses and buildings should not be built near the street in order to have more space for people to walk and to grow trees. Building's owner should devote some space to extend the walkways.
020102   Able to decorate houses to support BMA's policy in environmental preservation for tourist attraction. Give cooperation in house decoration to make Rattanakosin Island a tourist attraction.
E100113 The area should be more green. Trees should be pruned not cut down. Residents and shop owners should be encouraged to "green" the area more.
020901   Cars more than 10-year old should be inspected to reduce exhaust emission and to improve the traffic condition. Cars in good condition will decrease the level of pollution. It's up to individual's consciousness. If he has, the traffic problem can be relieved. My assistance is to maintain a good condition of my car, to give advice on pollution reduction to my friends.
021304   Do not litter canals or rivers.
021602   Car owners should not use their old cars in order to reduce pollution and help reduce the present traffic congestion.
070312   Don't discharge untreated wastewater into the river.
080204   Don't use leaded petrol.

CONCLUSIONS

Traffic congestion is apparent and easily perceived. Heavy traffic also accentuates other problems; air and noise pollution and visual intrusion being clearly and closely connected to it. There is, however, a wide range of problems that form the context within which road traffic issues are conditioned. Urban migration, economic and political power of the primate city aggravated by state centralization, and "consumerism culture" specifically "car culture" are just a few well-recognized examples. The underlying causes for these social concerns include weak political wills, absence or ineffective implementation of integrated policies and planning, administrative complacency, insensitivity of local governments, misguided measures, etc.

Bangkok, very much akin to many other cities in developing countries, faces four main problems, namely, urban poverty, inadequate provision of infrastructure and services, deterioration of the urban environment, and a weakness of local government administration.1 These problems have been tackled by various measures, and perhaps with a varying degree of success. Participatory approaches to development could prove a promising alternative.

It is, however, easy to preach participatory approaches to those who have changed their mind set to the needs of the present day when the values of democracy are widely shared. Although they may not form the majority in the society yet, their proportion is growing. But at the other extreme position of the scale, stand not many people either. Rarely heard is the voice of those who would absolutely oppose participation, or defend the position with great conviction. The sceptics and the unconvinced seem to occupy a large portion of the statistical pie.

Participatory approaches, similar to many other noble ideas, are not problem-free, when it comes to application. Participation could be used as a manipulative device. Planning and work implementation could be carried out in the name of people, whose ideas and suggestions are used to decorate or embellish the development process. Participation then becomes a pretence, or even a manoeuvre for political or economic ends.

However problems still persist, even participatory approaches are carried out in good faith. Common and justified questions are queries such as how do people know about the wider implications of their ideas and of official policies; common stakeholders are just interest groups, hence their interests are likely to be narrowly focused and even myopic; people are unprofessional and may be uninformed about the most modern methods of operation and technologies; etc. Therefore professionalism rather than populism gain more credibility in the eyes of many people.

It is undoubtedly true that people's views have limitations. But so do the views of others, be they professionals or bureaucrats. In fact there are many other arguments that form part of debates for or against participation. They are well documented both in a scholarly and a practical fashion elsewhere2. This report is not intended to add fuel to such debates among various advocates rather to illustrate two principal points, namely, (1) how urban development in general and local planning in particular could benefit from participatory approaches, and (2) an alternative action plan for local transport planning.

If urban development is rightly seen as part of social change as a whole, the efforts for the intended outcome should not be confined within institutions as in the traditional development paradigm, whereby the institutions are providers and the people recipients. People themselves constitute tremendous resources in several terms, i.e., in terms of physical/intellectual inputs, in terms of political, social support, etc. The resources are, however, not always in the ready form, but potentially available, like mineral deposits. It requires appropriate means to utilise them. The action plans (A and B in Part I of this report) suggest certain ways for the proper use of people as resources, on which the authorities could capitalize. The plans, however, do not provide any all purpose ready-made formula to practice people's participation in urban development administration in Bangkok. They could serve as an initial framework of conduct. Further experiences could help modify future actions, to be culturally more sensitive, economically gainful, and socially dynamic. Furthermore, the alternative action plans for people's participation certainly do not pre-empt any other measures to achieve good governance. They could also be integrated into the overall framework of institutional reform and social advancement.

Experience from the project clearly indicates that people's ideas and suggestions are extremely valuable. Their value is not just in being basic raw information from which professional planning is to be extracted, but more importantly, it is in providing sound proposals in their own right. Evidently many of their proposals, as formulated in the action plan, prove to differ from other official plans or commissioned studies. Their characteristics, *inter alia*, are the emphasis on the demand management side of solution, and not so much in the category of new infrastructure provision, which entails high cost and calls for time-consuming projects. The marked difference could well reflect a practical value of people's perspective, and therefore has a high possibility of implementation.

Regarding ideas, which are not in the form of direct proposals, their value could be of twofold. First they could sensitise planners in policy formulation. Secondly they express articulate wishes to be translated into action. Both aspects can be looked at as a synthesis between the people and the professional. As an analogy it can be compared with the relationship between the person who wants to have his/her house built and his/her architect. The former has ideas about the form and the functions of his/her dream house; the latter has knowledge and skills to transform them into a reality. For the best results possible, they need to engage in dialogues. Both entities then progress towards mutual illumination. And this perhaps describes the heart and the success of people's participation.

Endnotes

[1]   Nigel Harris, op. cit. pp. 28-32.

[2]   Two examples to suffice the point are one, a highly scholarly work of Michael Lynch, 1993. *Scientific practice and ordinary* action, Cambridge University Press, the other less academic in nature is Alan Irwin, 1995. *Citizen Science*, Routledge, London.

BIBLIOGRAPHY

The list is limited to those publications referred to under the section "Suggested Readings", in Part I.

Asian Development Bank, 2000. *Asian Cities in the 21ˢᵗ Century: Contemporary Approaches to Municipal Management,* Vol. 4 : Partnership for Better Municipal Management.

Manuel Castells, 1983. *The City and the Grassroots*, University of California Press, Berkeley.

Richard Gilbert et al, 1996. *Making Cities Work: The Role of Local Authorities in the Urban Environment*, Earthscan, London.

Ministry of Interior and Deutsche Gesellschaft fur Technische Zusammenarbeit (GTZ), 1999. *Public Participation: Approaches in Urban Development Planning and Management*, Decentralisation of Physical and Urban Development Planning Project, Bangkok.

Om Prakash Mathur (ed.), 1999. *India: the Challenge of Urban Governance*, National Institute of Public Finance & Policy, New Delhi, 1999.

UN-ESCAP, 1995. *Urban Forums: Report and Proceedings of the Workshop on the Use of Urban Forums as Consultative Mechanisms for Urban Planning and Policy Making*, 19-21 September, Bangkok.

UN-UNDP, *Empowering People: A Guide to Participation*, UNDP, New York, n.a.

The World Bank, 1996. *The World Bank Participation Sourcebook*, The World Bank, Washington, D.C.